OUT OF THE ASHES

Frieda Hughes was born in London in 1960, grew up in Devon, and after living in various parts of England and Australia now lives on the Welsh Borders. She wrote and painted from an early age, and for many years has been a painter and children's writer. She received a NESTA Award in 2002 to help her work on *Forty-five*, her portrait of her life in 45 poems and paintings, the poems from which were published by HarperCollins in the US in 2006. Her most recent work, *Alternative Value*, includes both poems and paintings and was launched by Bloodaxe in 2015 at an exhibition at London's Belgravia Gallery. *Out of the Ashes* (2018) draws on her four previous poetry collections with Bloodaxe: *Wooroloo* (1999), *Stonepicker* (2001), *Waxworks* (2002) and *The Book of Mirrors* (2009).

FRIEDA HUGHES

Out of the Ashes

BLOODAXE BOOKS

ISBN: 978 1 78037 403 1

First published 2018 by
Bloodaxe Books Ltd,
Eastburn,
South Park,
Hexham,
Northumberland NE46 1BS.

www.bloodaxebooks.com
For further information about Bloodaxe titles
please visit our website or write to
the above address for a catalogue.

Supported using public funding by
ARTS COUNCIL
ENGLAND

Cover design: Neil Astley & Pamela Robertson-Pearce.

Printed in Great Britain by Bell & Bain Limited, Glasgow, Scotland, on
acid-free paper sourced from mills with FSC chain of custody certification.

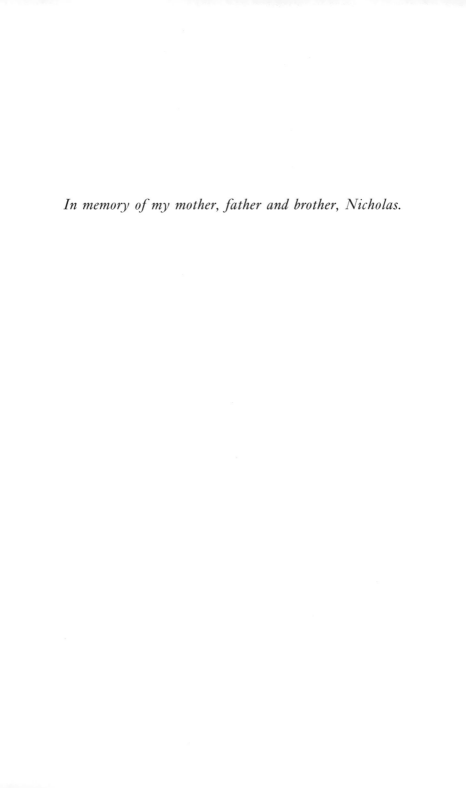

In memory of my mother, father and brother, Nicholas.

ACKNOWLEDGEMENTS

The poems in this edition were selected by the author from these four collections first published by Bloodaxe Books: *Wooroloo* (1999), *Stonepicker* (2001), *Waxworks* (2002) and *The Book of Mirrors* (2009).

CONTENTS

15 *Out of the Ashes*

from **WOOROLOO** (1999)

32 Wooroloo
32 Farmer
33 The Favour
35 Operation
36 Foxes
37 Changes
38 Hysterectomy
39 The Shout
40 Spider
40 Thief
42 Fish
43 Caesarean
44 Fire 1
46 Ghost
47 Granny
48 Three Old Ladies
49 Frances
50 Rosa
52 Winifred
53 Kookaburra
54 Bird
55 Dead Cow
55 Damien's Other Cow
56 Giraffes
56 Tiger
57 Birds
58 Readers
59 In Peace

from **STONEPICKER** (2001)

62 Stonepicker
63 Playground
64 Visitants
66 Fear
66 Dr Shipman
67 The Wound
69 The Little War
70 Communion
71 Beauty 1
72 Beauty 2
73 The Birdcage
74 Phone Call
75 Myra Painting
75 Hospital Waiting Room
77 Landmines
78 Mother
78 The Dying Room
79 Man Starving
80 Lunch
81 Endometriosis
81 The Writer's Leg
83 The San Francisco Fire
84 Salmon
84 Beetle
85 Crocodiles
86 My Face
87 Left Luggage
89 Silence
90 Bagman
90 Breasts
91 The Signature
92 For Ted and Leonard
93 The Last Secret
94 Conversation with Death

from **WAXWORKS** (2002)

98   *Introduction*
99   Madame Tussaud
101   Medusa
102   Pandora
103   Damocles
104   Medea
107   Circe
108   Rasputin
110   Samson
111   Sibyl
112   Rumpelstiltskin
114   Thor
115   Sisyphus
116   Houdini
117   Malchus
118   Cinderella
119   Jezebel
121   Malvolio
122   Hippolytus
123   Durga
125   Job
128   Nebuchadnezzar
130   Sweeney Todd
131   Salome
132   Vlad the Impaler
133   Morgan le Fay
135   Echidna
136   Nemesis
138   Sawney Beane
139   Arachne
140   Prometheus
141   Honos
142   Lucrezia Borgia
143   Satan

146 The First Horseman
148 The Second Horseman
149 The Third Horseman
150 The Fourth Horseman
152 Lazarus

from **THE BOOK OF MIRRORS** (2009)

154 The Book of Mirrors
155 Stonepicker and the Book of Mirrors
156 January
157 Stunckle's Night Out
158 The Sign
159 Self-examination
159 The Cure
160 Woman Falling
161 Stunckle Goes to a Party
162 Preparing the Ground
166 Puberty
166 Stunckle Sings
167 My Mother
169 Harpist
170 Message to a Habitual Martyr
171 Stunckle and the Book of Mirrors
172 Love Poem to a Down's Syndrome Suicide Bomber
174 The Problem
175 Two Women
177 Stunckle's Cousin
178 Gift Horses
179 Stunckle's Wish for a Family
179 To the Victor, an Empty Chalice
180 Here We Begin
181 Stunckle as Eyeglass
181 Stunckle's Truth
182 The Idea of a Dog

183   Nearly Fifty
184   Stunckle's Uncle
184   Assia Gutmann
186   Three Views of a Car Crash
189   The Reason for Not Being
189   Poet With Thesaurus
190   Things My Father Taught Me
191   Firstborn
192   Letters
192   To the Daughter I Never Had
193   To the Daughter I Could Not Be
194   Childhood Photograph
195   Sleepwalking
196   Nesting
197   Doll
199   Food Fight
199   Second Thoughts
200   School Doctor
201   Orphan
201   Potato Picking
203   Verbal Warning
205   George
206   George Examines
206   My Crow
207   Slowly Recovering Crow
208   Oscar Flies
208   Oscar Sleeps
209   The Trouble with Death…
211   Pheasant Running
212   Pheasant Escaping
212   Dead Pheasant
213   How It Began
215   Letter-bomb
216   Endgame

217   For Nick
218   Eulogy for Nick

223   NOTES

Out of the Ashes

In the beginning, when I was a child, the words used to claw their way up through my thoughts in times of stress, or unhappiness, or puzzlement, and ball themselves into a fermenting mass that I would then scribble out on paper when the pressure became too much, and I had to make space inside my brain. Happiness never had such a reaction, because being happy did not make me feel insular, neglected, unloved, sad or angry, or any of the powerful emotions that drive a poem into existence, like dragging splinters out of skin to effect relief. Sometimes an observed injustice, or an act of cruelty, would set off the spark for a poem.

Being happy, or simply content, was to be more relaxed – unless driven by *extreme* happiness, by perhaps falling in love (when clichés become a real danger), or achieving some longed-for goal, in which case emotional intensity would help to sharpen observation and condense ideas into poems.

So, when I was a child, I wrote a lot of poems, not thinking about my parents (Ted Hughes and Sylvia Plath) being poets. Poetry was simply an aspect of life, unquestioned as such; poetry was just what my father "did". Poems were mainly learned at school, and the rhythm and rhyme so popular at the time would whirl around in my head, finding objects and experiences in my imagination that they could attach themselves to, which would in turn contribute to my own poems. But the thing that made me *really* want to write poems was the feeling of being "other" than everyone else; of not fitting in somehow. When I wrote poems, the poems became a good reason for being alone, and I was good at being alone – being alone did not frighten me, because poems – and stories – were my friends, and I found that writing them gave me perspective; poems most of all. Poems were my language; short and portable, and the prism through which I reflected my perception of reality and the outside world, whereas stories were born of my inner world in the furnace of my imagination, and took far longer to write.

Boredom was another driver; I remember a notable visit from my American grandmother, Aurelia Plath, when I was, I think, 13. We had a meal at the George Hotel in Hatherleigh in Devon, where I was later to work as a waitress. I remember my grandmother, father, stepmother and younger brother, and recall the two others who were there. There was no conversation that included a teenager, and I was bored beyond belief, experiencing a feeling of something that disturbed me terribly; it was the sensation of time slipping past me, time that could not be got back; time that was disappearing without being any use whatsoever. I had a little notebook with me to put down ideas, or thoughts, or poems, or maybe because it had a pretty cover and carrying it around made me feel as if I had a life raft. And I had a biro.

As the boredom crystallised and the sensation of time passing uselessly became so unbearable that I could hear it like a wind in my ears, words began to form in my head, gathering like a storm, wanting me to be useful. I began to write; it was a rhyming poem about a hermit and began 'Far along a river's run / On the outskirts of a town, / Lived a hermit all alone...' And it got worse from there. But, it didn't matter, I was "doing something" and in doing something, even if it was no good at the end, I was practising for all the things I might write later, that would be better. I filled tiny page after tiny page; the urgency I felt was ferocious, my focus unshakeable.

Food arrived, but I didn't want to eat, because I couldn't eat and scribble down my thoughts at the same time. I was racing time, my appalling writing filling the notebook, and when I was told to put it away I had it on my lap beneath the table and carried on writing; the words were all there, waiting to be spun out of me like a web, and the resentment I felt at being told to stop because it was rude to write at the table built up inside me as if stoked in the furnace of my frustration. Even a visit to the loo was for the purpose of scribbling more. Couldn't they see that the words wouldn't be there when I came back to it, if I stopped now? The words were waiting, and they didn't wait for long before evaporating.

In my mid to late teens I wrote even more poems, carrying them around in a folder as if they were somehow a talisman, or would act as a lifeboat to save me from drowning. I liked to have them with me as often as possible, to work on at any moment that I wasn't doing something else. I still do that.

I submitted a wealth of these poems for my English A Level at 18, because the addition of "other" creative writing could improve our grades. Many years later, meeting up with one of my old English teachers, John Batstone, a man I held in high regard, I was reminded of this when he said: 'You submitted 96 of them! And they were all GRIM.' I consoled myself that this didn't mean they were actually bad, even though after all these years what he'd really remembered was the sheer number of them.

But by this time the importance of my parents' poems had been brought home to me, as they were both on the school curriculum. I had to get special dispensation to avoid "learning" about their work on the basis that, if I did badly, it would be unbelievable, and if I did well, it would be thought that I had cheated. This latter point was brought home to me when my father gleefully announced that if I had to study his work – and the work of my mother – then he could help. He anticipated a father-daughter bonding that was sadly not to happen, when I explained that I would very probably be accused of cheating, and that in any case, his idea of his own poems, and the examiner's idea of his poems, would probably be two very different things. No, I would have to study unrelated poets, and that's what happened.

After that, I made sure that I didn't read any of my parents' poetry... a fact that my father's sister, Olwyn Hughes, demanded I keep secret, as, in her opinion, I should know every poem my parents ever wrote. She was so vociferous on this subject that she drove me further and further into my resolution because, as much as it might shame me, I didn't want to be "contaminated": whatever kind of poet I was to become, I wanted to be my *own* poet, and if others were destined to compare me to my parents as they inevitably would, saying that I was surely influenced by them, then at least I would know they were wrong. I wanted to know that my voice was my own, for myself.

Once, in my late teens, my father asked me what I thought of a poem he'd written about a hedgehog. I began reading, got as far as the third or fourth line, and remembered my resolution. I made my excuses and, ashamed, handed him back the poem as if it had scalded me, leaving him somewhat bewildered.

However, from time to time I would show my own poems to him – occasionally eliciting longed-for praise – so that he could tell me if something didn't work, but to get it right was for me to find out for myself.

By the time I was in my early 20s I felt that I should spend more time on my painting, drawing and short stories, since the field of poetry seemed a little overcrowded with members of my family, but poems still leaked; I kept them in a large shoebox under the bed.

At this point I saw a publisher in London with my drawings and paintings, and they asked me to illustrate a fairy story or fable for children to give an example of my skills. I chose to illustrate my own story about Oscar, a baby dragon who resembled a pig, but developed into something incredible. This prompted the publisher to ask me to write something for older children instead, so I came up with *Getting Rid of Edna*, which was then, ironically, illustrated by someone else because my aunt Olwyn was agenting the book and made the deal. She agreed to the publisher's choice of illustrator without telling me. To my dismay, by the time I found out, it was too late to change anything.

However, it was my first publication, and it had been accepted under my married name so the publisher didn't initially know who my parents were. It was then that I decided my own name was the one I wanted to see on my own book because my marriage was in jeopardy. It gave me the impetus to give up work, put myself through art college, and write a second children's book, *The Meal a Mile Long*, which this time I illustrated myself, as I did with the one that came next, *Waldorf and the Sleeping Granny*, about a witch school and the relative from hell. More children's books followed, and I was delighted when Chris Riddell agreed to illustrate them because I loved his work. In the meantime, I kept away from poetry because of my conviction that I would never be judged on my own merit. Although I did have one poem published when I was 15 under the pseudonym Rachel Hailey, it didn't feel like "me"; it felt all wrong.

From the age of 24 to 34 I metaphorically sat on the lid of the shoebox beneath my bed in which I kept all those poem-leakages, and concentrated on painting and writing children's stories, supplemented by working for an estate agent in the UK, and then as cartoonist for the *West Australian Magazine* in Australia when I moved to Perth in 1991 at the age of 31. My parents were strangers there, and I experienced an undeniable freedom from any noticeable public consciousness of their work; in Australia, it was as if they didn't exist, certainly not in my world.

In January 1994 I moved with my then partner G to a little hamlet called Wooroloo, several miles out of Perth, on the way to Northam and the mining town of Kalgoorlie in the outback. There was no literary life among the stones and the kangaroo paw plants, but I had found somewhere I truly loved to be.

Except that, in order to get there, I had to decorate the previous house and ready it for sale. It took several weeks, during which time I did no writing and painting, since I was now entirely focused on moving; the idea of being able to indulge in uninterrupted painting and writing once I'd got to the new house consumed me. G worked out in the bush for five weeks out of six, so there was nothing he could contribute.

The new house was a small kit home (a bungalow out of a box) on fifteen acres with a creek going through the middle, populated by lizards, snakes, ring-necked parrots, cockatoos, and the occasional family of kangaroos; it was my little slice of heaven. This was the place where I would paint, write my stories, and build my future, coming back to the UK every few months to sell what I had been working on, as my publisher and most of my art clients were in London. Instead, this was where I collapsed.

It began when G had his three children, two boys aged 11 and 15, and his daughter, aged 13, over to stay from the east coast. We'd only just moved in, so there hadn't even been time to unpack my work from the boxes stacked beneath the verandah of the house, as I longed to do: the desire to get back to work had become all-consuming; I was pining. Not to write or paint for so long made me feel as if I'd had my wings sawn off.

Nevertheless, I succumbed to their pleas to accompany them on a two-week trip down south to Margaret River, where we would stay in a rented house near the beach.

I asked myself: how could I work for so long on decorating the old house; the buying and selling of houses, then the flooring and preparation of the new house, and not want to take two weeks' holiday with G and his children? Surely I could spare the time? And it was only two weeks…besides, we only had the one car between us, so I'd be shut in at home with my work, overlooking the creek and the valley and our little bit of woodland, with no way to get out and about. Except, of course, the idea thrilled me, and I couldn't wait for the others to leave.

Reluctantly, I packed, climbed into the passenger seat of the car, and resigned myself to the two-week delay of my longed-for return to work. As G drove us further and further down the coast I felt as if I was not in control of my own life. I'd made a boundary, then allowed others to drag me over it.

We'd been driving for about an hour when there was a *ping* in my head, like a guitar string snapping, so loud a sound that I thought everyone must have heard it, but they hadn't. After that *ping* I felt strangely breathless, tired and foggy-headed. But it wasn't until two hours into the drive, when we stopped for a break, that I realised there was something very wrong; my legs wouldn't move, and my arms felt like lead. I had no strength, and for a woman who had always been physically strong, this was alarming. (See 'How It Began' from *The Book of Mirrors*.)

G came around to my side of the car to see what the problem was, and I tried to explain except I had no idea what to say. My voice was as exhausted as my will to move; I was literally too tired to speak. G didn't seem to understand that I wasn't kidding. I forced my arms into movement, hooked my hands beneath my left knee and tried to prise my leg out of the car; it was like trying to move parts of a dead body.

Eventually, with G's help, I managed to get both legs out, then had to ask for his help to stand. I wanted to sink to the ground because my body felt too heavy to hold up, my exhaustion was overpowering. And this is what I was like for the holiday – immobile for most of it, and barely mobile for the rest of it. I told G and his children that I must have some kind of strange flu, although secretly I was certain that it was psychosomatic and would improve as soon as I got back to painting and writing.

Fortunately, it poured with rain for two weeks, so the fact that I could barely walk became less important than it might have been. However, I couldn't do anything useful either; reading a book was impossible, because the words didn't make sense. It was like reading a foreign language, over and over, hoping the words would sink in and find a meaning; already dyslexic, this new affliction pushed understanding of a sentence completely out of my reach. Concentrating on any task at all was nigh on impossible; my focus would simply slide off the idea of anything as if it was coated with Teflon.

When I got home, thinking that my strange affliction would vanish once I was reunited with my watercolours and computer, I couldn't get out of bed for days, and finally I had to drag myself to the doctor, miles away, again and again, first for several blood tests (I have a recollection of 36 of them), then a psychiatric test (which declared that I was incredibly sane), and a brain scan (which confirmed that I did have one). Getting myself to appointments was a challenge; I'd start out two hours early to get through a 20-minute drive during which I would have to stop at least once, to sleep – and the sleep was non-negotiable, more like a sort of sudden unconsciousness.

Eventually the doctor announced that, having exhausted all other possibilities, I had ME (myalgic encephalomyelitis). Delighted that I had a diagnosis, I asked him for some medication so I could get on with my life. At this point he explained that it was also known as chronic fatigue, and there was no cure; I could be afflicted for life, although the degrees of that affliction might vary.

I'd heard of chronic fatigue, and associated it with over-worked city-types who needed a good holiday, so I'd always thought of it as a bit of a joke, but now I wasn't laughing.

In the following months I discovered that rest didn't help, and other people couldn't help; in fact, their presence only exacerbated my periods of unconsciousness (and so G and I soon separated), and that I had to work at my own speed, in my own way, which often meant working during the night, because if I was awake I'd have to seize the opportunity as there was no telling when I'd be awake again. No matter how I tried, keeping normal hours didn't work for me at this point.

When it began, I was awake for around four hours a day in 20-minute stretches. I had to work out a way to exist within the framework that had been unexpectedly imposed on me; I found that my fury at being incapacitated only made it far worse, and that any kind of stress completely exhausted me – and when I say stress, simply being asked if I would prefer tea or coffee was too difficult; I couldn't imagine whether I wanted either and the mental struggle to do so would bring down unconsciousness like a blackout blind. So, I was faced with a few life choices, and one was this:

Given my time constraints as they were now, what would I want to have done with my life, I asked myself, when I got to the end of it? The answer was that I wanted to write what I wanted, and paint what I wanted, and not fear the opinions of others. Acknowledging my new limitations, fear of the opinions of strangers somehow seemed unimportant. For ten years I had banned myself from writing poetry, or painting big, flagrant, colourful oils, because I felt I'd be too exposed, too easily aimed at... But, when the alternative was to have lived a life without even attempting these things, I realised it was always up to me to make the changes...

I stacked a pile of scrap paper on the kitchen table around which I now lived, and began to write poems. Once I'd written something, I put it in a second pile, although I often couldn't read through to the end of a page before my brain ground to a halt, at which point my mind simply wouldn't present a proper understanding of the words. My thoughts were short, so the phrases were short, and the poems were short, but now that I'd released myself from my self-imposed poem-exile, it was as if I'd uncorked a bottle that had been ready to explode; I couldn't stop. I did the same thing with oil paints and small canvases; I placed the materials ready to work, and, in short periods of time when I was awake, I'd daub something – anything – but usually a quick picture of the sunset, as the sun set very quickly, and I didn't have to imagine it; it was right outside the window. Those creative efforts were the foundation stones of the nearest thing I'll ever get to a recovery. Everything I did then, and everything I do now, requires an act of will.

As the weeks passed, I noticed a small, incremental improvement in my abilities, with occasional short bouts of energy, after which I would of course collapse. But sitting at the kitchen table to write, I really felt I was *doing* something, and the more I did, the more I felt I was investing in my future. I had to believe this, even if it proved to be wrong, because working in hope gave me energy that working in despair did not.

At one point, having already written *The Think in the Sink* and *Rent-a-friend* before I became ill, I wrote *The Tall Story*, but I wrote it "blind", as I couldn't read it back to myself to make sense. By the time my story was accepted for publication and I received the proofs, my ME had improved to a degree, but I still couldn't read more than a few words before my brain closed down. So, I persuaded a friend to check the spelling, and read the story aloud so that I could hear it, telling her not about being chronically fatigued – as I had told only G – but that I was dyslexic; something else I didn't often share. *The Tall Story* was published in 1997.

Later, during a visit to England, I showed a stack of poems to my father, and asked him to make three piles: good (could be published in a book), could be worked on (then published), and bad (find another shoebox). I didn't want him to comment other than that, because I still harboured the desire to be free of his poet-influence, yet his was the opinion I valued above all others.

The poems in the good pile were enough for a book and a half, and so I created *Wooroloo*, my first poetry collection, with poems set in the environment in which I lived, and allegorical stories into which I often placed myself, as I was shy of being too open about some things; I'd never had the practice. 'The

Shout', for instance, is a poem apparently about sheep to begin with, but is really about me questioning my mother, when I'd wondered if she had worried about her effect on me, should she live... 'Fish' is about a boyfriend I'd guessed was still in love with a previous girlfriend, so I persuaded him to give it another go...although poems that did not involve my thoughts about others were very much more direct, such as 'Hysterectomy', an operation I was obliged to have as a result of years of chronic endometriosis, which was then followed by the need for yet more surgery...

Autobiographical exposure in this way was new to me then, but I found that the poems gave me a voice, whereas before it seemed to me that everything happened in a vacuum; incidents in my life, good or bad, simply festered through lack of acknowledgement when I should have given them recognition for their influence on who I was.

These poems also helped to contribute – with the new paintings that I was doing, which were bigger, brighter, oils on canvas – to my sense of myself, and that in turn contributed to the amount of time I was awake and able to function. I still didn't tell anyone about my chronic fatigue; I didn't want pity, or to be thought of as "less".

Wooroloo was published in 1998 in the US, the year my father died, and in the UK the year after. My father was elated when he heard that my first collection had been accepted in the US by the behemoth that is HarperCollins, and it was only after this that I felt I could finally read my parents' poetry, although finding poetry books in Perth wasn't as easy as I'd thought. I ended up with a slim volume written by each of them, which I read with curiosity and some apprehension – only to find that we seemed to share nothing in common, just as my father had always maintained. The only commonality in some instances was the subject matter, because I grew up among animals in the country.

Stonepicker followed *Wooroloo*, drawn from my favourite poems – evolved from the initial mass – and poems I wrote following my return to the UK in 1997, when I first discovered that my father had terminal cancer. The title-poem is about a woman (it could just as easily be a man) who collects grievances with which to abuse those she considers to be at fault for the ills in her life, as she believes herself to be blameless. The last two poems in the book, 'The Last Secret' and 'Conversation with Death', deal with my father's death on 28th October 1998, and the poem 'For Ted and Leonard' deals with the death of my father's collaborator, the artist Leonard Baskin, on 3rd June 2000.

Examining aspects of my life through my poetry, or observing the actions of others, be they friends, acquaintances, colleagues or politicians, for the purpose of a poem, gives direction to my thought process – I am forever analytical.

After my father's death, there were things that happened in my family life that beckoned a stronger embrace of allegory; I needed to express myself, but to do so directly made me feel too exposed altogether. I had already written 'Sisyphus' in my *Stonepicker* collection, which was my observation of my father never being allowed to put down the metaphorical corpse of my mother, and that, as what I call a "seed poem", was the beginning of my third collection, *Waxworks*.

Waxworks hammered its way out of me; the energy that the characters brought with them was powerful: I visited Madame Tussaud's; I re-read the Bible from cover to cover (only having done it once before, to compare testaments), and I scoured my books for my favourite mythological and historical characters, from Rumpelstiltskin to Merlin, from Sweeney Todd to Cinderella, and from Samson to Thor. The Four Horsemen of the Apocalypse (Revelations 6) at the end of the book reflect certain problems impinging on my consciousness at the time: suicide bombings, foot and mouth disease in 2001, genetically-modified grain that is unable to reproduce, and the war between men who want to cover up and contain their women, and the women who want to be free.

I became 'Madame Tussaud', the collector of figures for the book. In the second part of this poem, which is almost a separate poem in itself, I wrote about the potential destruction of my parents' wedding rings: I'd been told that my father – who, now that he was dead, could no longer speak for himself or be reasoned with – had wished them cut in two, so my brother, Nicholas, and I could have half of each ring.

When we discovered this, Nicholas and I were surprised that we hadn't been consulted. He begged me to get them back before they were destroyed, which I managed to do, but the person who was going to slice up the rings wrote a letter stating that if there were a curse on her returning the rings she sent that back to me also. Secrets and lies seemed to abound, and I dislike the harbouring of these; I had to set them free, and I set them free in *Waxworks*.

Although my own experiences were the ingredients for many of the poems, I feel very strongly that 'Vlad the Impaler' wrote his own poem, and 'Nebuchadnezzar' is a poem about the time Tony Blair was Prime Minister, attempting to find a use for the Dome in London.

The poem 'Nemesis' is about a London party I once attended, where I was introduced to someone famous by his first name. He was so famous that my host, who almost mentioned the man's surname, bit it off as unnecessary before he got it out. But I had never seen a photograph of the famous person, who was also famously rude, so in shaking his hand I politely enquired after his surname in order to avoid assumptions that might be incorrect, whereupon he pulled his hand from mine in a rather brusque manner, waving me away with a dismissive gesture as he turned his back on me, and replied 'It doesn't matter,' thereby igniting a poem.

Rasputin, on the other hand, is a modern take on a timeless con-man. He is based on the historical figure, using a real situation – one that happens over and over again, when people trust their life savings to the person who will take everything, and leave them with nothing.

This book felt to be truly shaped out of molten lava, and led me to write *The Book of Mirrors*, in which my fascination with consequences takes an even stronger hold. I also created a bit of a family, who are blind to consequences, life lessons, and the well-being of others: Stunckle is so named for being Stonepicker's uncle, and in turn, has his own uncle ('Stunckle's Uncle') and a cousin; very soon they may have their own book.

A few months before the publication of *The Book of Mirrors* in 2009, my brother committed suicide, and I found myself immersed in writing poems about his death as I tried to ride the sharp-stoned rapids in the river that I felt I'd been tossed into. Two of these poems made it into the book, and like the poems about my father in *Stonepicker* and the Four Horsemen in *Waxworks* – poems that I consider important to me – they went in at the end.

There are also poems about letting go and avoiding conflict, 'To the Victor, an Empty Chalice' and 'Endgame', because life is too short, as well as poems about my teens, because I realise that as I have grown older, I have become more curious about my own past, something I avoided when younger because it was often simply too difficult, or too painful, or too recent. But I am fascinated by what makes us behave the way we do – myself included – and how some people evolve through questioning themselves and admitting their strengths and weaknesses, when others disguise themselves and fail to realise their potential as a result, becoming members of the 'Stonepicker family': I always want to know 'why?', 'how?' and 'was it worth it?'

I hope that *Out of the Ashes*, my selection of poems from *Wooroloo*, *Stonepicker*, *Waxworks* and *The Book of Mirrors*, goes some way to illustrating my journey so far.

Not included are any poems from my autobiographical collection, *Forty-five*, published by Harper Collins in the US, or any poems from *Alternative Values*, my illustrated poetry collection published in 2015 by Bloodaxe Books, in which poems about love, life, death and planning ahead, among others, are illustrated by abstract images visually describing my emotional reaction to the content of each poem.

These two books, although also descriptive of my experiences, observations and history, stand apart because their specific identities define them as individual.

FRIEDA HUGHES

Wooroloo

(1999)

Wooroloo

Wild oats pale as peroxide lie down among
The bottle brushes, a beaten army, bleaching,
Life bled into the earth already, and seeds awaiting –
Stiff little spiked children wanting water.

Above the creek that split apart the earth
With drunken gait and crooked pathway,
Kookaburras sit in eucalyptus. Squat and sharp-throated
They haggle maggots and branches from ring-neck parrots.

I have watched the green flourish twice, and die,
And the marsh dry. In this valley I have been hollowed out
And mended. I echo in my own emptiness like a tongue
In a bird's beak; my words are all gone.

Out of my mouth comes this dumb kookaburra laugh,
        How my feathers itch.

Farmer

Slim, beautiful thing he was, like a dropped angel.
Eyes huge, set amazed in his face,
He wondered at the universe;
Strange man, tree watching.

She caught him young. Hollow vessel,
She saw his ownership of things, and wanted;
Observed his weakness early, and nailed him to the floor
With an unexpected daughter.

Hooked, like a mouth-torn trout,
He was held fast by the cry and spit
Of little childhood begun so sudden, so surprised.
Mother felt her job was done,

Had used her womb like a weapon. Now her words
Beat him down; he was harvested in his own fields.
His bruises bloomed, those blue roses sank their stain
Beneath his surface, made him dumb with pain.

He learned to be silent.

In his head he hid. Green grew there,
And rocks cracked hot in the sun; his landscape
Was knitted by lizards and boulders of sheep.
There, she could not find him, or snap a bone

With the thought that made her child,
It became her stone. Its heaviness outweighed her.
At last she left him,
Strange man, tree watching.

The Favour

The man with the sickle
Is searching for something.
He wades fields of thick gold crop
In house-high boots that do not disturb
A sharp hair of grain.

But the little things
Hear him coming.
Rabbits freeze,
Their sad blood is oil
On his metal blade.

Still thirsty,
He crosses a continent:
They are crushed in their slums,
In their fallen towers,
In their earthquake.

He has to find them fast, find them first,
The old ones fight hardest,
They know him well,
Have seen his face often;
Not one of them wants him.

Except the suicide in the back room,
Dangling impatiently,
Her shoes off,
The chair fallen.
She is waiting.

It isn't her time
So he breaks the rope,
Gives her soul back,
Forces her to breathe it in
Like smoke.

But she isn't having it,
She begs to be a sacrifice of no significance
At the end of a twist of hemp.

This time he takes the too-soon spirit,
He puts her in his pocket for later.

He is so rarely loved
That he likes to keep those ones close.

Operation

My head is lead, neck all bent
When I try to lift this melon,
I have no control. The stalk drags its fruit.
Sullen, my mind's eye at the bed edge
Watches me helpless.

I am a damp moth with wings sticking to sheets,
Folded in creases – my chrysalis is split open
But a tube anchors me,
Leaking into my blood from a plastic bladder,
I am diluting.

Struggling to connect my parts,
A leg slides to the floor, it is only minutes now
Until they lock the curfew door, and leave me staring
Into the dark at the needle
Sewn into the open hole in the back of my hand.

So, I hold still the medicine ball
That sags between my shoulders and sit,
Like a top-heavy hinge; I am
A small clown in open-back gown,
Pale face and blood spots across my belly.

Each wound hole is knitted with a single stitch,
Closing the small mouths of protesting flesh
In two bloody pouts. I am unhooked and escaping,
Each arm a dead albatross rooted in a shoulder blade,
Each leg a tree dragging mud and earth.

I am a monster of pieces.
My spirit watches from the corner
And follows at a distance;
Doesn't recognise its home.
As I leave, I am alone.

Foxes

Christmas night. The three of us
Are eating steak and salad without
A relative between us, beside us,
Or even at the end of a table
That would sit twelve, if we had chairs.

He appeared at the floor-deep window,
A sudden little red thought. Lost,
When we looked, like a name on a tongue-end,
Never certain. Ear tips like a claw hammer,
Face like a chisel, then gone.

He was back, two bits later, whippet body
Wanting steak fat. Half grown,
His small feet black as match heads,
His nose not able to let
The smell of meat alone.

His very presence begged us for a bite,
Hungry in the houselight. And there she was,
Just as motherless; his sister,
Coming for dinner,
Threading the field like a long needle.

Changes

I wore another woman once;
She arrived in a bucket of dye,
And began as a blond streak
With a blush like a carrot.

There I was, face beaten by the cold
In a cut-off winter, with a six-foot hearth
Burning paper left by the last supper;
The boyfriend, his girlfriend, her boyfriend

Eating without me,
Their chicken bones left to spit and crack
With the books and the bills and the savings certificates
Of total strangers. I was warm for two weeks.

This woman woke,
The streak had spread, her head was red,
Her face like stone. She swept up her ashes
And dressed differently.

She borrowed me awhile,
In fact, I had to take me back
When she married without me
And left me holding the husband.

It was only a very small box,
But the bottle inside poured me out
And coloured me in; I was found at last, in my own skin,
Still wearing her creases.

Hysterectomy

I want nothing left.
No threads stringing eggs like small beads
Across the bottom of an ice box.

No second chance will wear my face,
And cry out to be born
From another woman's belly.

No stolen child of mine will know
His blood was borrowed, and his third mother
Was a brittle thing, seen through like glass.

My disease will be stripped out
Like the rotten lining of a leather coat,
And, neatly sewn, I will end here.

The Shout

Black sheep crawled from its mother's blood,
And staggered.
At first, it wasn't obvious the colour was wrong;
It didn't match.
Mother's job was done,
So they buried her.

Animal's legs found earth and rooted.
Mud upwards,
It grew and flowered, still wearing its mother's stain:
Strange stalk
In a field of yellow daffodils, found itself unmatched
And unrelated.

Earth-bound knotted thing, tore ligaments and talon
From dirt, and moved forward.
Roots dragged and stumbling, it opened its mouth
And out of it
Like the dead echo of a stone now dropped again,
Came its mother's shout.

Did you die for me?
Was the voice in your head, that uglied you,
So loud it would drown me out?
Tulip-red you took yourself to bed
And slept without me. Precious dream,
More than I was, took you from me.

Dead, you are made over.
Your face is painted in again,
And faultless, you walk.

Spider

Her hunger fresh,
She feels for the tendon
Where the fly is protesting,
Its stuck feet like the motor
Of a small boat
Burning out in weed.

The wire is tight,
The fly, bedded in a soft blanket,
Is dead
With a goodnight kiss.

Thief

It was years before I dug my grandmother out
From where her shadow lay, like a bloodstain
Beneath the black stones I had
Weighted her down with.

Her smile was crooked,
She had been dead awhile.

Back then, when, as a small child, I watched,
She said she had come for my mother: She beckoned,
A sweet promise coated the lips that kissed, like honey,
But her eyes were empty already.

When I reached my two-and-a-half-year-old hands
Into those holes, I found nothing
Behind the sounds her mouth made,
But her tongue flapping.

'Come live with me!' she cried,
Nostrils spread above like nose wings
As if her face would take off from its neck-end
Like a ghastly bald crow.

Seeing my mother was a shadow not hearing,
And my father not found
To know his daughter was disappearing,
I became blank, wiped clean like a pale sea stone.

I made myself as hollow as a dead tree,
Not worth having.
My days were as lost as marbles; even my name rolled away
To disappear between a crack in the floorboards.

I was stolen after all, and in my silence
The visitor grew dim. Uncertain. Receded like a dull fox
Just before dawn, barely left a scent behind
On door frames and bed linen, then was gone.

Fish

What have I done?
I have given him back.

Thrown away something
That glittered for me.

Let it slip through my fingers,
It needed to breathe.

This fish never had my face
In its eye, it was always averted.

His lost dorsal fin was knocked off
On a rock, somewhere,

He felt its absence. Someone else
Was swimming with it now.

All I did was point out his bald back
Where he was left wanting.

Now he must decide
If he can wear it.

His worry is, it may not want him,
Being now an independent thing,

With its own trout attached.
And I am gone. A picture

Under skin of water, like a twin
Broken with the falling stone.

Caesarean

That's the trouble with these babies now;
They take one look at that hot, wet hole
And hear the traffic and the screaming beyond,
Even only for a taxi, and they try
To climb right back up again.

A father adds up the cost already,
He is showing pennies and cents
To a dilated vagina and hoping
The kid can count.

With its feet on either side
Of its mother's gaping manhole
And with the nurses beckoning, the child
Is hanging on to the placenta
Pretending to grow there.

Until suddenly, the door opens.
Not the trapdoor with the head-clamps,
But the side door with the hip-hinges,
And it all begins.

Fire 1

It missed me twice.
The first time at the Candlestick stadium
It caught me in its black rain.
Its sky was sick with trees and gagged
By walls and wooden floors and small dogs,
Swallowed whole.

The second time,
I sat under my tin roof
And heard the ashes rattle in the gutter. Made a wish
With every one, like coins in water.
Its footsteps levelled oat fields and skinned trees,
Quick as locusts, hot as branding irons.

This time it shouted.
And I was out. Furious,
Its voice burst fat beneath tree bark
And the possums froze in their little ash-pose,
Brittle bones pinned black
In their burning hollow.

Still, I didn't hear.
It was louder now. The neighbour's sheep
Were cooked in a field corner, and the chickens blackened
Beyond possessing even a beak or claw to make them birds.
The garage buckled in pain,
Its window dripped from the window frame.

Fire called again.
I was too far away to see
My studio twitch with its disease.

It began with a small red spot
That flowered in the floorboards,
Its anemone danced, and the music
Was the crack of wood applauding.

I wasn't in the audience
When fire ate the metal roof like a rice cracker.
Left only crumbs, a dead fridge and bottles
That had mated in their molten passion,
Where once there was a corner of a room
Beneath a sink.

Fire was there when I returned,
Watching from smoke-stumps, and barely satisfied.
In bare, black fields rose twisted squares
That were sheds once. And the studio
Lay perfect on its plot, a fresh dug grave
Punctured only by its own ribcage.

But the house remained.
All the fire hoses had been and gone
And left it clean. Soot ran right up
To the verandah where fire had stood calling
And not been heard. Even the water-tank
Was fresh.

Fire saw this.
Above the tank grew a vast tree, rotten with life
And crawling things. Fire had hollowed it out.
Still it burned. Fire drew itself together
For a final shout, and the tree exploded,
Left the tank tangled in limbs and emptying its broken cup.

Fire was still laughing
Three days later when, in the dark –
Like musical notes left over from a large opera –
The last flames echoed from their stumps.
Eyes unslept and lips curling,
Still eating.

And now I treat blackened saplings
With water drippers and a plastic tube,
As if the land were some mammoth animal
On life-support for a small cat.
And the last leaves of the tallest trees
Have this new death-voice
As their bloodless shells clatter.

Ghost

Lost, he came to watch me,
Wanting something.
Fearful of discovery
As if a dead man
Had anything to hide.

He touched me, like a blind man
Learning woman for the first time,
Fingerprint by fingerprint
Until he held my echo
In his hands.

He took my breath between his lips
To fill his hollow lungs,
And watched me live –
As if he could unbury
How he died.

Piece by piece he stole me
Until I had all gone.

Granny

Mirror, mirror, on the wall
Who is the least dead
Of us all?

You loved me not, just saw
A copy of the face
You gave birth to.

Wanted to catch it without warning,
Not like last time,
When it slipped away for burial. Defied you.

Chewed through its own ankle like a fox;
Left its foot in the trap
Like a lucky charm.

But I wouldn't have been that way;
Didn't have the mother-guilt,
Didn't need the approval.

Sought love from you,
But got spiked by bitter
Spearheads from your railings.

Wasn't going to bleed for you.
Wish I could cry,
But couldn't lie like you.

Three Old Ladies

Beaks open, magic cracks
Like eggshell in their dry throats.
Three marsh birds spit blood at their hospital sheets.

At night, their ghosts clatter,
Given life in the breath of old women. In the day they sit,
Each at their own bedside, visiting themselves over and over.

As long as death does not call
In his unbeatable, terrible voice
Their unfleshed bones may snap beneath their sugar paper.

Their lights are pinched
In the fingers of dark
That are putting them out.

They will use their last green twig
To keep that light burning,
Or it is all for nothing.

Frances

Haired like Beethoven, she would never
Have heard of him. Her cry was a heron,
Mud-stuck and staring up at the ceiling.
Her hands, each like a small, separate child,
Dropped things. I would collect them for her.

The spoon from the soup, or the tissues
When her blown nose had filled the sheeting.
Her nurse-cry was indignant, surprised at her need.
As representatives of her state, and the only means
By which she moved from bed to chair,

From sleep to sleep, she called on their duty,
Her smell hanging like a damp flag,
And they 'didn't fucking know
The meaning of the word "help"'.
Every movement caused the knot

That locked her two knees together,
To drag pain from her twisted hip. Each jolt,
Another tooth pulled, each tooth
From a mouth a mile wide; too big to see each side.
I found out her real fear, when she asked for my help

Because there was a picnic, with children,
Two hours ago. Where were they now?
And this bed was the wrong one,
Which one should she sleep in?
And a tap dripped in a bathroom I could not reach.

In her sleep she woke, and could walk.
She remembered everyone she once knew;

Their laughter slapped the walls
Of our white room like a hand clap,
And the nurses with their soup and their pain,

And their ground-down powders,
Should have been the dream. She smiled at me,
Spoke my name, eyes as big as the glass balls
That were her spectacles,
Before she slept again.

Rosa

She is sticks of seen through blue
And pale yellows of skin. Texture
Like a camel's lip; she needs softening.
Rosa with the broken hip, is mending.

Beneath the blanket scrolling from the angle
Of her knees, she hides the hollow drum
That beat out forty years alone,
But for her son. Dark hair, dome-scraped

Wrapped in anorak. They had lived together
Until his wedding at forty-one.
Rosa smiles at me with her sheep's eye
And tells me how her new daughter is blind,

But is so clever that she can find
Her way to the shops on the bus,
But could not have a house guest,
She excuses her son.

Two girls wheel her home.
She is to be planted with her climbing frame,
And allowed to flower. But a cold hand
Has cracked a pipe upstairs, like a glass straw.

One snap in the roof space, and a small murder.
Hungry water has unrolled the wallpaper
Like tongues, and the ceiling full of heavy juice,
Has fallen. The sofa floats.

Oranges are planets in the fireplace,
And the last of her son's books
Left in his old bedroom,
Have opened like anemones.

I meet her by the lift
As they wheel me from x-ray.
Her light is out. Her beak silent.
Her good eye and her bad eye stare

At a spot in front of her,
In equal quantities. In that spot
Are all her things; her wet slippers, her chair lift,
Her Christmas biscuits and the floating oranges.

Two months, her son says,
Before her house is ready.
Those two months are a wall
Her hip might not climb.

She knows how hope taken
Could snuff out a candle like hers,
That dances in the growing dark,
In death's breath, and at night, in her own.

Days are only moments before her, she is carved like wax.
I ask what she sees in the floor,
In her stunned hours.
'My house,' she replies, 'My floating oranges.'

Winifred

Frances and Rosa watched her progress
And wished for her stick.
Winifred on her third leg.
Its black rubber boot beat out her hobble
To the neat, white toilet,
Where she could pee, privately,
No nurse watching her jowled cheeks open
Above a bed pan.

Determined crab, she returned herself
To her dry mattress and lay,
Only a few minutes
Before she was gone again.
Frances and Rosa called for the commode,
Their four-footed frames
Were metal twins at each bed-end.

Winifred rose for the last time at lights out.
She was free for home tomorrow,
At ninety-six she was an escaping pigeon.
But took a wrong door and found
The nurses' bathroom. No wall bars.
Surprise crippled her as she hit the floor.
When her hip snapped, her wings were broken
And she was wheeled back to us.

Bones awry, hands twisted up like paper,
She sat with the face of a distressed dog,
Remembering she hadn't peed yet.
No one understood,
Except, that having fallen in the bathroom
She was, of course, relieved.
Her dark beads burrowed
Further beneath their white folds,

Trying to hide her efforts
Not to pool in her seat, like melting ice.

Kookaburra

So big in life, head like a chopping block,
Beak like a carving knife,
His hysterical voice cracked branches, his laugh
Stripped bark from the wood-borers.

But in the twilight something got him,
So close to the house I should have heard.
He was left like a taunt, a dead bird
By an empty chicken run.

Now his dusk-stained feathers rock
In their dead grass cradle,
His bitten body is the flame
From which these moths escape.

That beak is buried in the sucked-out skull
Where eyes were lost in another mouth. His small crate,
Ant-eaten already, has ribs open like rafters
To welcome flies, and his wings rest like two open fans
Beside him.

Stripped of what made him,
He is only a fraction of his noise.

Bird

Flip-top with brain
At the beak back;
Mouth so wide open
Houses would disappear.
Continents cringe, curl their toes
And hang on to their oceans.

Maw with a jaw as wide
As whatever enters; small mice,
Large cats, or middle-size rats
With twisted whiskers.
Its call hallows the black
The brings silence.

And the body bears feathers
In its quiet; its little soul sleeps,
So small in its twigs.
If it yawns, or belches,
There is a city in there,
With its lights on.

Dead Cow

Balloon-cow at roadside
Offers up her odour
To the flies that skate
The currents of her openings.

Their creature voices in her bloodied dark
Are met, and echoed in their eaten corridors;
A last breath, as her flesh
Offers up its children.

Damien's Other Cow

Dead-headed, her withered lump
Has been separated from its stump.

Her petals have been peeled
By all those little black bodies he employed

And paid in sugar,
To secrete their young

Into her stolen vessel.
Egg-laid once, his blue sun

Calls them to its hot wire,
And kills them.

Giraffes

Heads huge, two sky ships sail the branch.

The enormous windows of their eyes weep with tree dust;
Black carbuncles, ink-filled,
With shutters feathered like lashes on a woman.

Green flags hang from one starboard,
The other, mouth empty, takes them
With a kiss like a collision.

Their faces knit whiskers,
Their extensions dance above crack-built bodies and below,
Legs dangle; bone splints breaking for each step,

Every movement a swing of slow anchors.

Tiger

Tiger is born of tiger.
Looks like tiger.
Eats the same meat,
Does not complain
About its stripes;
The black slices through
Auburn red
Like sun splitting thin
Black slate.

Does not complain
It looks the same.
It eats to become
Is father, to become
Its mother.

Birds

The poet as a penguin
Sat in his snow-cold, nursing
The egg his wife had left him.

There it was, born of them both,
Like it or not. Rounded in words,
And cracking open its shell for a voice.

In the blizzard,
Beaten up from the arctic flats
Were the audience.

From the glass extensions
Of their eyes, they watched
The skuas rise on the updraft,

Every snap of their beaks
Like the tick of a knitting needle,
Hitching a stitch in the wait

For a rolling head.

Readers

Wanting to breathe life into their own dead babies
They took her dreams, collected words from one
Who did their suffering for them.

They fingered through her mental underwear
With every piece she wrote, wanting her naked,
Wanting to know what made her.

Then tried to feather up the bird again,

The vulture with its bloody head
Inside its own belly
Sucking up its own juice,

Working out its own shape,
Its own reason,
Its own death.

While their mothers lay in quiet graves
Squared out by those green cut pebbles
And flowers in a jam jar, they dug mine up

Right down to the shells I scattered on her coffin.

They turned her over like meat on coals
To find the secrets of her withered thighs
And shrunken breasts,

They scooped out her eyes to see how she saw,
And bit away her tongue in tiny mouthfuls
To speak with her voice.

But each one tasted separate flesh,
Ate a different organ,
Touched other skin,

Insisted on being the one
Who knew best,
Who had the right recipe.

When she came out of the oven
They had gutted, peeled
And garnished her.

They called her theirs.

In Peace

My lover is dead, at last.
His head in my lap, his hair
As yellow as grass; his weight
Has kept me rooted
For his creek and his green.

Only his parrots and kookaburras had speech.
In between, fires made them
Little more than fox dinner,
And my trees withered.
With them, I lost my words.

All that knee-bent, coil sprung
Taut voltage, that made my brushes work
And my paintings bright as flame,
Has become earthed in the dirt. Stuck in rock.
My sentences are the roadside crosses.

Language got small here;
Syllables and consonants fell off the plate
Like too many peas, left
Just two or three to play with,
Over and over. I should lay flowers.

Much loved, that loneliness,
My man-in-the-cupboard.
But he had no voice, just
A body to be buried in,
Had he not died first.

Stonepicker

Stonepicker

She is scooped out and bow-like,
As if her string
Has been drawn tight.

But really, she is
Plucking stones from the dirt
For her shoulder-bag.

It is her dead albatross,
Her cross, her choice,
In it lie her weapons.

Each granite sphere
Or sea-worn flint
Has weight against your sin,

You cannot win.
She calls you close,
But not to let you in, only

For a better aim.

Playground

They were practising themselves,
Trying out their little fists.
But a punch was nothing new,
It did not have that resounding shock
Of being just invented.

Big girl shook her short hair.
Hot and wretched,
She was boiled in her skin
And might unpeel
At any moment.

Her blue wool and grey skirt
Were dragged and twisted round
Her fleshy mountains, and
Small girl laughed
As agile as a goat, and wide-eyed,

Using words that stuck
Like gum on shoes,
Better than a fist and leave a bruise,
And all the legs of little boys
Like bars, and all their noise

Filling up the big girl's head
With memories of ridicule
That would repeat again, again,
For years inside her brain. She knew
One thing must stop it now

Or face it every day at school.
She watched the other girl, mouth wide,
Laugh and point, no matter
How she cried. Her idea was simple;
Take the laugh away.

The small girl didn't scream at first, until
Her bloody lump of thigh
Was bitten out and left.
No more than a mouthful, it silenced laughter
Among the children in the playground

Long after.

Visitants

Trees crabbed in their leaves,
Bundled black like old women.
Hunchbacked and planted,
Breathless,
They waited for sound.

Houses, subsiding like three-storey
Headstones in a burial ground,
Were blind to the street.
Their windows and doors
Shut like eyes and mouths against noise.

And it came.
Hauling its body of notes
Through the night air,
It came. Dragging its throat behind
Like invisible rope, it came.

When it arrived, fixed as I was
Like a camera, I could picture nothing.
The screech repeated as if
To pick itself out and
Hold itself up for a look, at nothing.

For a year, the study window
Was my waiting eye
For the dying goose, or a cat
Beneath a slowly rolling truck;
Anything that could make that spindling cry.

Until one night, beneath my car,
An invisible windpipe broke open
And scraped asphalt with that same howl;
A bloody-ended, shrill stretch of raw meat,
And no murder.

And then suddenly,
Winter-bushed and city-blackened,
Two foxes scrambled from the wheel arch,
Baiting each other like lovers. Breath like smoke in the cold,
Their mating cries
Untangled between them like a joke.

Fear

He sits on the bed-end, my black foot
Foul-mouth friend. Breath like hot bitumen,
His smile is tangled in those rotten teeth,
His hand upon my ankle like a clamp.

He, heavy jailer, holds me for tomorrow
When they cut out the pain,
Take away the lost flesh like the secret body
Of a dead cat wanting burial, and stitch me back again.

I have made him up of my own mud and clay and blood.
I stapled him together. Gave him life.
He is the only one to touch, and sit, and wait with me,
In my dark, in my room, until it's time.

Dr Shipman

God is a doctor. His secret adores him, as close
To his skin as his beard – hedge-cut
To hide all but his letterbox – and his eyes,
Counting down corpses on his abacus
Ten at a time.

The strength in his poisoned needle
Adds inches to him. His power to take,
Or to leave until later,
Must be the joke that splits apart
His foliage to laugh.

Weeping relatives make him
Their Wailing Wall and he watches,
All death certificates and consternation,
From the superior vantage point
Of his mounting body count.

God, undiscovered in his disguise,
Plans his afternoons so death
Is between lunch and dinner,
Like a snack; a little something
That feeds his empty hole.

When God is found out for being
Someone else, he is thrown into jail.
But he still thinks he's God as long
As he holds the answer to the question.
God locks his tongue in a box, and swallows it.

The Wound

She carries her wound,
It is carefully disguised
Beneath her underclothes.
It is still bleeding.

It is her mother's fault,
When her mother imagines
Her child might not be
Blameless.

It is her father's fault,
For not having a hole
Like hers, so
Not understanding.

It is her husband's fault,
For wanting
To stop up her pain
And the pain, stopping.

It is her sister's fault;
Calling her untaught,
When her pain has made her
Very taut indeed.

She lies down with her pain.

It is the sword in the bed
Between her and her lovers,
And her friends and her sister,
Her father and mother.

She sharpens it daily.

The Little War

Victim has turned on killer and
The two of them are arguing
Over a television. Killer took it
When the killing started, but somehow
Victim didn't die,
He came home to find
The contents of his house
Had moved across the street.
Now he wants his television back,
And his fridge, and his
Electric cooker but
No one has pointed out that
The power is down
And the generators are in the hands
Of the Russians again. All he knows is
That his fridge still wears
The alphabet magnets brought home
For his dead son. They hold
The last scrap of his wife's face
In a photograph,
Torn, and left beneath
The letter 'S' and
He is prepared to kill for it.

Communion

Ten years old, I was asleep. Dreaming,
I was dragged from the folds
That clasped me like a ring-stone,

And sat up.

My head refused to release
The people in it, rolling on my shoulders
With the weight of them.

A face was
Thrust into my face.
An urgent, unlikely face,

Not a house-face.
I must dislodge sleep to see it,
It might never come again.

My bald eyes struggled for it,
Wanting focus for
A fixing-point.

Ears. He had big ears.
And eyes astonished as my own,
That stared back, unblinking.

Fox met me nose to nose,
So close, his coal-tip was too soon
For a sharp edge.

I wanted to climb inside
His black holes, and stroke
His terror down.

Orphan four-legs, off to find a home,
Brought in to be shown,
Just once.

I was still
Embedded in him as
He was carried to the door.

Beauty 1

Picked brows and puckered mouth,
Pumped up with belly fat, and belly
Sucked in through a tube,
Through a hole in you.

The look has become the life. The bed edge
Is pushed further beneath the knife.
A little tuck, a little cut, are not a lot
From last time. Seventh, eighth or ninth time.

But the face is not the one you wore before
Your seventeenth birthday. Men hold it
In their hands, your lips, like petals,
Curling with tattoo. You have made

A thing that only is, if someone looks,
And looks, and looks.

Beauty 2

Italian waiter poured the water
As I waited. The seat opposite
Marking me out as if
I were naked.

I watched the couple
Led to the table beside me.
He had a face that
Thirteen-year-old girls

Would colour-copy twenty times
And pin to their walls, his many eyes
Like swords, polishing on their new breasts. She
Was the surprise. A nothing face.

Not bulbous, nor lumpy,
Nor scarred, nor strange at all. But blank
And plain beneath her mouse-cap of hair.
Hand-held, his looks dwarfed her.

She smiled. There was this
Pulling back of skin to let in light.
Her voice was a pounding river, where he swam
Over the perfect white stones of her teeth.

Her fingers were tiger lilies, dancing.
She was illuminated
Like coloured glass, and he
Was kneeling at her window.

The Birdcage

It is bright and gold, ring hold
At the top, for a chain.
A little girl is caught in its bars
As surely as the toy bird.

Each of them, perch-bound. One looking out,
The other peering in, but trapped
By those green and blue feathers and
The bead of a dead eye.

Not given to her, she must watch
Another child carry the canary
To a hot spot on the radiator
For its trick.

And there it is left, in the rising air.
The bird shudders as if life has just been
Forced back through its yellow beak
And into its small mechanical breast.

Its wings open, its tail spreads
And suddenly it is singing:
'I should have been yours,
I should have been yours.'

Phone Call

She's phoning again.
Hardly ever a man would call
This way. Even
A stealer of days would be
More of a javelin thrower.

But her voice is all warm
For the dog in you,
Word-beaten, daring to play again,
With the sucking child
And its rattle of scream.

She opens her mouth,
As big as the door of her house,
To let you in
With your toothpick
For the bits in her teeth,

And the pounding of train
From the back of her tongue,
Through the eye of the telephone.
And when she is done,
She is already calling again.

Myra Painting

Myra, Myra, on the wall,
Hung at last to please us all.
The little hands that painted you
Thought it a good game
To pick out your face in its frame,
And fill it in with their fingers.

In your own art, your skill is still
Buried with the children. Little unfound bodies,
Stuck inside your casing like you
Nailed down their mothers, hammering them in.
When the passer-by squeezed out the juice
From a fountain pen, theirs was the laugh.

All that is left are mirrors of ink,
Like black pennies, drying
Beneath your vacant lot. Outlined
In a square of white tape, like taping
The fallen body, they are a new installation,
And you have gone to be restored.

Hospital Waiting Room

Chipped from Meekathara mud
With a pick and mattock,
All his little parts baked together,
His skin of leather
As dug out as gullies.

His broken arm has brought him in
From the outback oven, his splintered limb
Tied up in the sling of a tea towel. Pain
Pins him to his chair, as if
He has been harpooned to it.

The watch upon his wrist
Ticks off its digital seconds;
Hidden in the blue and white check
Of his kitchen cloth, it is
A little bomb waiting to go off.

At three o'clock, we are woken,
Our stupor broken. The screeches
Of his sudden alarm have reached
Into the room's sky,
Pointing him out
Like the arrows of wind vanes.

He suppresses his cry, his tears
Funnel into his hide
Like rain in a creek bed.
This bushman beats desert to squeeze
Water from a branch
And a plastic bag,
But cannot gag the five-dollar clock
That straps his broken wing.

His other hand cannot help;
He is thumping the watch
With a cut-off stump and a bit of an elbow,
Three o'clock, three o'clock, three o'clock,
But his melon-end can't make it stop,
And his left hand hangs helpless
Beneath the watch band.

The large woman beside him
Unfolds, her fat forefinger
Traces her eye to the button
That switches him off,
And, for the first time,
His face unbuckles and opens
Just for her.

Landmines

The legs are waiting.
There must be places in Heaven
Where they are stacked fifteen deep,
Along with fingers and arms
From industrial accidents,
All waiting for their bodies to die
And come to find them.

I may meet up with
My womb again,
And a foot of colon that was severed
At its two ends
To become a worm in an Elysian field.

But every day I walk forward
I do not have to know
My legs have gone on ahead.

Mother

Three, like stones, her children lay
Smooth, round and heavy in her lap, her little gods.
Kept her fearful and still, her hair pulled out
Thick by roots, blood made,
When he asked a question.
Wrist skin twisted black,
Each bone a pivot,
If she turned her back.

Sharply dragged, her pain was silent
For the heads she cradled.
But his white powder had a hammer-shout,
Broke those spheres like glass.
Their shattered faces were perfect moons
A moment before his blunt language
Beat their edges out, and he made them
Wrong forever.

The Dying Room

Mother, father, no child,
Made the space between them
Into a hard thing.
A boulder in the bedroom, washed clean
Where they cried. Secretly, and separate.
Each afraid of the other.
Of their invisible baby.
That rock, their burden, should have been a daughter.

And in the dying room, the children gather.
Where Death does not need the language,
But picks his nails and cleans his nostrils
With shin bones small enough to knit with.
He knows they will come easily,
Because the cold seek warmth,
And even in his rot and tatters
He wants them most.

Dressed meat, their moons shine.
Tiny girls, not to know
Why brother lived. Never loved,
They grate until they stop,
Little clocks all run out and empty.
They clatter in their graves like hollow tins
And mother, father, no child,
Polish up their stone again.

Man Starving

The Saturday supplement had been stacked
And left. No one
Would pick it up and place
That man's face beneath their arm.

His black eyes rattled at the back
Of his deep burrows. Their whites
Were wounds in the newsprint.
They leapt up and got you.

He was four-legged like a dog, but
Not from having lost something;
His bones would snap
If he tried to upright his sticks.

His skull smiled up through skin,
Full lips of flesh
Had shrivelled and dried like worms,
His teeth were constantly naked.

And the cameraman, without words,
Had picked him up in his lens
And printed him out, over and over again.
We could almost hear him weeping.

Lunch

You sharpen me like a pencil,
Lighting matches just to burn them out.
Hiding your mud feet beneath the table,
You watch the children die in my face.
I see your hair is greyer now,
I have missed pieces of you.
Remember not to show your holes
Or I am ferret in your earth.
But now I see your face is cleared like water,
Filtered through the stones you give
For me to throw and make
The circles on your surface.
We collect our lost parts.
Between us, they polish like opals.

Endometriosis

It crawls up through the groin.
Nail hooks pick out steps in soft red,
Seeking places to implant
Like a cat, screaming and curious,
Trapped, too fat with feeding
To get out through the way in.

It takes root and flowers, its bloody petals
Falling where no wind blows to rid the earth-flesh
Of the shedding velvet, that clogs and gags.
The claw-roots run too deep to peel
From the hollows of the inside,
It must be made hungry to die.

The only answer is to steal its food bowl,
And cut out the unborn children.

The Writer's Leg

His body parts knew better
What his talent was. Contentedly, they stretched,
Grew, and waited, growing hairs.

But he was a boy then, and the blood
That pumped him like a piston never let him sit
Long enough to find it.

His arms and legs drew lots to see
Which one would win the right
To let him know and make him listen.

'Not me!' his right arm cried, 'he needs me
For his very purpose, my fingers dance,
Their music is the thing we fight for.'

'Nor me!' his left arm cried. 'As you can see,
I am the balance for all those computer keys.
Without my digits, he does not add up!'

The legs met each other at the knee,
And conferred. They decided on skates.
The first to give in, fall off, or buckle

Would find itself free
To make this boy listen to his head
Above the sound of his own feet, running.

The blind car drove backwards
And hit him hard, so he noticed.
Left him lying there, broken.

His left leg apologised from its
Stitched skin and splinters
For not giving the right leg a proper chance.

Fresh and bloody from its third operation,
Its mouths grinned up at the head and said;
'Now sit and write something.

Where others use a pencil,
You have me. I am your gift.
So use me wisely.'

The San Francisco Fire

The Forty-niners played the fire
At the Candlestick Stadium.

The men were on the field
When the plane flew over,
Tail trailing flag advertising a sale.
And the oval skylight was shut as if
Night had clamped it.

So many people with radios
Now switched them on. Watched
The game at the same time
They heard the flames on interview.
Eucalyptus burns best, and the hotel exploded.

The commentary took trees down, ten at a time.
Someone scored a touchdown,
And we knew the people leaving
Were homeless already.
Then came the slow, black snow

With their furniture in it.
And their toys and their photographs,
The water from their swimming pools
And everything in the garden shed.
The crowd cheered. The fire won.

And we walked to our cars in our hundreds,
With the black dust of burned homes
Thick on our chests and shoulders,
In our hair and on our forearms.
We carried the shadow as one.

Salmon

The boy stood, adolescent,
In the river gravel, holding
His dead salmon. Its eyes
Begged up at him, with clouds in them,
And his own eye.

By degrees, he sank. His ankles
Were disappearing and still
The fish lay cold in his palms.
The gravel pebbled against his
Soft, white man-flesh, and in it
Rolled a hundred nested embryos
And he, still clutching the father,
The carcass.

Beetle

The little beetle curls his mouse
Into a basket. Tucking in paws,
And tying in the tail.

The mouse is amenable
By way of being dead
From a beetle-bite.

The beetle burrows into
The soft centre of mouse-belly,
And lays out her embryos like jewels.

Squirming with the separation of cells,
They grow, split and feed, on their casket,
Becoming maggots.

They hollow out their bloody stink-nest
Of dead flesh, which still wears
Its mouse face,

Fattening to fall, and become beetles again.
The first ones out
Get to eat their brothers and sisters.

Crocodiles

Like squeaky toys, their noise
Makes children coo. Their little eyes
Like balls of wide surprise,
Are bugged for mother with
Her mouth of nails. And she,
With limbs like trees
And skin of knotted bark,
And weighing all a ton,
Collects her little ones.
Pouch-rocked in her throat,
She sets them free again
In water, with a tongue
As gentle as fingers.

My Face

As I sleep, other people
Wear my face. It is still
Worn out when I collect it
From the bathroom mirror
In the morning.

I haven't dared a surgeon yet,
To pick off the lines and
Cast adrift the boats
Of my eyes and nose
And mouth.

But in the forty years
That I have seen them all afloat,
Without a cord or chain
To anchor them between my ears,
Above my chin and throat,

My skin spiders and flesh mites
Have been knitting up each
Facial twitch and scratch. They even caught
The creases from my first laugh,
When I spilled out of the womb.

Longest worked on, it must
Run the deepest. A straight rope
From voice box to navel. And if the line
Is taut enough, you will hear
It still plays the same note.

Left Luggage

He was born like a box,
Put together with sides
Of mother and father and
Everyone trying to read
The label of contents.

For a long time he looked after
Each of his occasions, even
That moment when his wife left him.
It was hung from a hook
On one of his walls.

He used to stand inside himself
Sometimes, and have a look.
Dangling in his gallery, it rather
Overshadowed his smaller memory of
Their meeting at the fishmongers.

Between their beginning and end
Was a Nepalese mountain,
The heal for a scar from a straw-jump;
A hidden spike,
And drinks at six weddings.

It was easier just to smell fish,
And forget her.
Even his brother's first bike
That he stole, was parked
Up against the punishment.

The day came when all the weight
Of a sumo was accommodated in his frame.
He no longer rattled with expectation.
His digestion was slow, and his belly dragged.
Something must be shed, to move him on.

His internal shelf was weighted down
By his book of self,
Everything was written in.
For weeks, he fingered his
Own pages, trying to work out

What to lose and what to keep,
And what to look at longer.
He read himself over.
Finally, when he had remembered everything,
He got up for a cup of coffee.

Leaving all his chapters
On a park bench,
He realised that
He didn't have to go
Back for them.

Silence

If I am silent for long,
Maybe twenty minutes, you will
Fill that quiet with the sound
Of your own traffic, a dog bark,
And the voices of all the people
That inhabit your mind and
Make up your memory;

Your several brothers and sisters
Sitting in an elm tree,
The branches cracking beneath their
Gathered weight like hot fat,
The two wash-hanging mothers
Tossing their words like sock-balls,
To and fro, across the fences at the back,
And the first and last partners
You ever made love with.

By the time I speak again,
You may no longer believe me.

If I am silent for years,
You may even bear my children,
Marry my husbands and mourn
The death of my parents. You could
Chop trees from my hillside,
Imagine the smell of my lilies, and complain
My shoes do not consider your feet at all.

If I never speak,
You could invent me completely.

Bagman

The cloth is torn
And stripped, and laid
Like splints along his legs.
Tied with string
To keep him in,

He is heaped. A sack
Of spilling clothes, all rubbished,
That rise and fall with sleep.
And in the rain, his fraying ends
Struggle to escape their knots and twists,
The man inside his chrysalis.

Breasts

Scarred beneath their bags
Of heavy silicone,
They were mountains,
Shored up and sharpened,
A handful of the mind's mud
At a time. Those breasts

Weren't for a limp sweater,
Or a bra size more than
Two saucers. Those breasts
Had purpose. Men's eyes
Would unpage magazines
For a sight of them.

Melissa was no longer
Required to speak.
Her breasts could talk.
They had a language
And everyone
Understood.

When at last she made the photo shoot,
She gently placed her breasts
Of shiny plastic flesh
Upon the table for
The cameraman,
And left.

The Signature

One for you, one for me,
The books are being
Divided between us. Leftovers
From a library where, at night
In the dark, or between
Dinner downstairs and the bathroom,
Sticky fingers would find
Whole volumes stuck to them.

Each book is opened, and there
She has written her name. A mother
For you, a mother for me,
Another for you, another for me,

And suddenly, a small square
Cut from the page corner where
Her ink had dried.

Perhaps the coat pocket was
Too small for the whole story,
But just big enough
For the nail scissors.

For Ted and Leonard

The bird was broken.
Cracked open. Split like a pod.
From inside its Siamese halves
Its two fathers looked up
At the sky they had made,
And the creatures that had crawled
Out of the pit of each
Sibling mind and lived,
Breathing, with heartbeat,
Even as their own failed.

Each pulsed like a lung
In his half-shell,
Blowing the beak like a horn
To make it speak; their shared mouth.
Until one ceased. The other, listened
In disbelief. Waiting, waiting, waiting
For the next word, using his one claw
To draw, mostly himself, as if

The dead half would suddenly
Return to write the narrative,
With stickled fingers pushed into
The other bird-claw glove, pen-held
And laughing at his joke. Instead,
In silence, nothing happened.

The half-bird, still attached
To his memory of being whole,
Found it harder and harder
To think about anything
Except finding his lost part.
So at last, he left
To go looking.

Crow rocked in the dirt, in the wind,
Blameless at last.

The Last Secret

Death
Is the elephant in the room.
We can't speak about it, even though
It stalks you. Thorny-haired,
Its eyes of nostril turning always to you,
As if you have some special smell.

It stalks us next, but for now
It wants you first.

You don't want its word
Anywhere, or in our mouths.
Its presence makes us dumb.

So, it is the elephant in the room.
In my sleep, I take a gun
And shoot it dead. But in the morning
Its weight is at our feet again,
Wanting to be fed.

Its body is on the hearthrug
More faithful than any dog,
And beside the table, and
Beside you in the car, even though
I sit there; its mournful, stupid eyes

Unable to avoid you. Slowly,
Its breath is stealing your breath,
Its heavy feet rest upon
The altar of your chest. Tonight
I am going to kill it again.

Conversation with Death

Death has come to have a look
At his work.
Sitting by my father's coffin, fingers
Linked in his lap like any doctor,
He is smiling.

'You took him too soon,'
I say.

'It wasn't easy,' he tells me. 'Every time
I found a way to get him,
He slipped out of it.
That first time, I was sure
The cells I chose would do it.
I watered each blessed seed.
I visited daily. My flowers flowered,
But I found he could uproot them
With almost a thought. Each day
Was stolen from me. Even when
I had him by the heart;
Tried to stop it beating,
Held it fast with my two hands, it was as if
He climbed inside his own crawl space
And picked off my fingers, one by one.

'You could have left him longer,'
I protested.

Death frowned. 'To take some
Poor soul, car-crashed by the roadside,
Or with bullet holes and
A leg blown off, is easy.
There is no grace in that.

'But to take a Greatness, who fights
With all that accumulated excellence,
Derived from a full time, even
Had in a short time,
Is an art.

'I could have had him in his thirties,
I wanted him then.
I have wanted him all along.
If I told you I nearly
Lifted him off a train when he
Was only forty-two or forty-three, and a
Little arrhythmia was going to be
My percussion's end
To his ebb and flow of corpuscles,
Could you not see
How lucky you are
To have had him for longer?

'I let him ripen on his tree
Like a heavy fruit. But to wait
Until his stalk broke, in his eighties
Or maybe even his nineties, to have him
Roll into my lap like a ripe fig,
Would have ruined me.

'To take him at the peak of his
Perfection, when he was at his
Escaping most cleverest, meant
I really got to achieve something.'

Waxworks

(2002)

.

Introduction

Waxworks is a collection of poems written about figures from mythology, fable, the Bible and our criminal history.

In some cases the characters speak for themselves, about their own lives. In other cases I have lent them a new life, basing it on the framework of their old life and bringing in elements of the modern world to extend, parody or reinvent them. They are new characters born of their old selves, with new histories.

I have attempted to explore our human vanities, including anger, greed, love, jealousy, sorrow and regret. I hope I have made no judgement upon them, since they make their own and that is their purpose.

At the end of the book is a brief description of each of the actual characters upon which the poems are based.

Madame Tussaud

Marie Grosholtz has been shopping.
Among the Louis Vuitton handbags
She found Dr Crippen,
His moustache like a zipper
Fixing his lips together.

She uncovered Durga, cradling her corpses
In the discounted section
Of the Army and Navy,
Nails like penknives, blunted
By cutting Berberis for wreaths.

She met Thor in his bear-paw slippers
Commiserating with Loki
Over a vodka and tonic in a London club.
And outside, Houdini, swinging from a street-lamp
Screaming for a key to his padlock.

Already a collector of heads
For her library of faces,
She is putting together a family,
Gathering up the possibilities
And taking them home in effigy.

*

She is looking for fingers to fit
The two wedding-bands from her dead father's
First marriage to her dead mother.
He'd thought to have them cut in two,
Half each of each for Marie and her brother.

He'd thought a friend would care
For his two rings, and his two children
Who cried out when he died
To keep his last two pieces uncut,
When everything else had been torn up.

But Herse had already looked
In the baby's basket,
And was made mad. She returned the rings
With a curse for not being divided
As a father's last wish, by her little saw.

With other wishes for his children
Left undone, this was the only one
When stopped, would leave them something whole.
Marie thinks Sisyphus will do,
Or Samson, or Zeus, or Thor.

She has worked out their shapes,
And boiled their actions and vanities
Into their features. She will see how they fit;
When sculpted in wax
Her likeness sits among them.

She'll make a mould of Herse too,
When Herse has thrown herself from the top
Of the Acropolis. She'll paint on a face.
If her work be collecting biographies,
Then madness has its place.

Medusa

She is the gypsy
Whose young have rooted
In the very flesh of her scalp.

Her eyes are drill-holes where
Your senses spin, and you are stone
Even as you stand before her.

She opens her lips to speak,
And have you believe.
She has more tongues to deceive

Than you can deafen your ears to.
If you could look away, the voices
From the heads of her vipers

Would be heard to argue.
If you could look away,
The pedestals of your feet might move.

If you could look away,
The song from the cathedral of her mouth
Would fall to the floor like a lie.

Pandora

What has she got in her box
But photographs. Starched with age,
Imprinted with hands and faces
Browning as if tanned,
And smiling mouths, unrelated
By blood or friendship.

She never looks,
She knows them exactly
For their features. There is a dead mother
She never met, whose children
Are disembodied from their memories
By the box-lock and Pandora's grasp.

There is a father too, dead now, whose flesh
Is ashes even while his likenesses
Outlive him. Mostly unseen, uncopied,
Or unsent to his children. Pandora keeps
The charred package of his body
Separate from his photographs.

One day she may scatter the first in the fields,
But will she ever release the second?
Should she cast out her collection
She would cast out the world's evil –
All that filled her with asperity,
All that gave her purpose.

Maybe it has been so long now
That she and the box are interchangeable.
If the box were emptied

She would rattle like an empty tin
With one thing left in for alms,
And if at last she spoke,

That one thing left is hope.

Damocles

Damocles has been advising his sister
Against her three children.
She has confided in him
The injustice she feels
At being questioned.

Her brother answers.
His words describe her rights in keeping
What the children understood was theirs,
When she could not detach herself
From her apparent wrongs.

But she cannot convince them
Of her innocence, even
With the knives he has given her
To defend her protestations of truth.
Her sharpened edges divorce them.

Like dogs that cannot be unbeaten,
They've gone. They no longer want
What she warranted was theirs,
It frees them from hope
That she'll keep the promise she broke.

Nor is her secret safe,
She will sink with the weight of it.
And Damocles sees at last, the sword,
Hung above his shoulder-blades
By a thread from a horsetail

In the head of his sister.

Medea

When Medea's eyes observed Jason
Floundering among the Argonauts
For the Golden Fleece,
She knew she had the means
By which to marry him.

She could make the end of effort,
Of sweat and longing,
Seem as close as the fingers
On her out-held hand, if only,
If only he would hold it

And make promises. She gave him
The ointment to make bulls blind
And sang the song of persuasion
That stupefied dragons,
Until he had the sheepskin

Dangling from his two fists,
Dripping lanolin and ore.

Only to find it was bedding
For his two brats, and she,
The mother-to-be.

Jason feared this woman;
This sharpened axe
With an eye for the thing he carried
Between his thighs, and the gap
On her ring finger.

He thought he would cast her
Out to sea in a boat,
To be carried off by the current
So he could imagine her better,
Happier elsewhere. Begun again.

But she was forged from stock of steel;
Mother of metal, father
Unreasoning of foreigners,
Ploughing their bodies
Into fields for the birds.

She could not uproot
Her wish to be his wife, her very will
Demanded he adore her. She wanted
To obviate his speech and cast
His words of protest to the wind

Like broken pigeons. When Jason loved elsewhere,
While Medea still dragged in the shackles
She wished to bind him with,
All reason abandoned her
As he had.

She dangled her end like a rope,
From which she might hang
If he did not attend her
Frequently, for the face of it,
Among friends,

Keeping up appearances.
Until he lay down one day,
Too tired with trying
To unpick her like a deadly orchid
From his branches, and died.

Now she severed the children
From their attachment, with a knife
That looked like a pen
In the hand of a lawyer.
She did not care they could not

Be put back later, to crawl
Wriggling into their cold skins
To be hers again, as if donning a tunic.
Without them there would be nothing
To show she was less-loved or the loser.

Far cleverer this, than a poison gown
For his new bride, and her own death.
Or an ending to it;
Forgive and goodbye,
And move on.

Her brother beware,
Lest she descry
That he was the one overheard
Telling her story,
And be cut into pieces.

Circe

In the beginning, the child
Whose bandied legs became
The stalks on which you stand,
Played with a stick.

The stick in your hand
Was made magic by the grip
Of your fingers, as if it was
Conducting music.

But music did not play
The way the creatures did.
You found your childish toys
In the men you changed.

A bored movement made a goat
From the man who cut wood
Who laid his head in your lap,
Glad for a girl's thighs.

And the man who killed chickens
For your mother's table became the dog
Whose mouth of bloodied feathers
Slept at your bedside.

And your mother's lover
Walked out one afternoon,
Left his shoes to come back for
As if he would be back soon.

And a weeping rat
Scuttled the house
Searching the floor for its footwear,
Driven on by your laugh.

Now your stalks dance
To the faces of men, mooning
Beyond the stage-end.
You swing hip over knee

To stretch an ankle
And one man is a humping camel.
Your breasts shake free
From their silver cups

And one man shrivels up,
Until his ferret-face
Is all that hangs over
His dropped collar.

You no longer need a wand
To make animals of men,
Your body has become
The thing that makes men beasts.

Rasputin

He's selling God, you can buy the book;
Six dollars a bible. He sells life insurance
On the side and can do a deal
On a car for the cash and a ride.

His wife is pregnant again – each child
By a stranger, he says to the girls
Who want to understand his vast kindness
In taking on another man's burden.

If they looked a little closer they'd see
His face on each of the three, bastards
By rumour only, his wife undone
And left when he found another one.

But his eyes like pointy spears, darting out
From their almond greens, are looking
For anyone who won't ask questions
And move him on. What he has seen

Are the voids that women carry; their wounds
Wanting to be stopped up and gagged.
'Come sin with me,' he tells them,
'And my forgiveness will set you free.'

'God is embedded bodily, as if I have
Been marked out by the gift
Of his most powerful blessing and made
Immortal. My hands are magic.'

And his hands performed. They took
Houses, cars and chequebooks.
The old and the infirm came to him,
Their powers of attorney flapping

Like winter cloaks, eager to be given
To a man who promised warmth
In return for their investment.
When, one by one, cast out as empty,

The men and women stood up in only
The emperor's new clothes, they discovered
He'd been poisoned once for fraud, and lived,
As if God acknowledged his apology.

So this time they shot him.

Samson

Delilah thought her scissors would get him.
That he would lie in her arms, bewitched,
Then sleep, his long black hair
Shorn to the scalp of his magic.

She thought his muscles would waste
And weaken. That the pillars of his building
Would fall beneath the weight
Of her womanhood.

She imagined that his body, cut off
From what made it most beautiful
Would shrivel at its own ugliness,
Lost, without its lion's mane.

She had studied herself and seen
The root of her own vanity. She thought
His would be the same. That once uglied,
He would stay.

She took each of his tresses
And felled them. On the floor,
His tangles writhed and died, divested
Of the head that gave them purpose.

Samson woke from the soft nest
Of her thighs. His eyes
Took in everything. She smiled
And waited for him to topple.

'My weakness,' he said, stepping over
What had once adorned him, 'Was you.
But you have severed me from your lap
With your sharp edges, and now I am free.'

Sibyl

Sibyl and Herophile are playing chess.
They have before them
All the pieces they need
To work out a conclusion.

But each is wise to consequence;
Each has an eye
On the next move
In the head of the other.

Herophile had promised action
Based on a letter from
Someone, dead now. But Sibyl saw
Each undertaking made as straw

In the fire of Herophile's
Other intentions, blazing and gone
As wind-blown ash
Withers, and is worthless.

Now Herophile swears an oath
That the past, which Sibyl sees
Playing behind Herophile's cornea
As if her eye were the keyhole,

Is only conjecture.
Whereas she can clearly discern
Sibyl's purpose as being
One of argument and delay,

When Sibyl only wants to position
Her first piece, but Herophile
Is arguing and delaying, it being
Her move.

For as the game is not begun,
Neither is it won.
But stagnant, waiting, unended,
Always, always.

Rumpelstiltskin

Rumpelstiltskin wants a child.
Crumpled in on his face,
Hunchbacked and trailing his ears,
He knows there isn't a woman alive
Who would lie down for him.

Once he spun gold from hay
For a workman's daughter,
Three times, to marry her off
To a king who coveted her fingers,
All for the price of an infant.

Just for a game, to stop up her wail of protest
When he came to collect,
She must guess his name, he said,
And he would forgive the debt.
He limped off laughing, to wait.

But she caught him out; he was seen
Applauding himself as Rumpelstiltskin.
It took him years to unpick
His right foot from the earth
Into which his fury propelled it.

Rumpelstiltskin wants a child,
He is too old to adopt, even as a non-smoker
Working from home. He could teach it
To spin gold from straw
But no one wants his skill any more.

He is searching hospital bins for anything
With life left in. He can make
A silk purse from a sow's ear, a clutch bag
From a severed hand, or a descendant
From a cut-out ovary.

Thor

He was tempted with love tokens,
He was fed morsels that bewitched the palate,
He was sung to by a voice
From the throat of one of

God's most blessed instruments,
And for a moment
He put down his hammer and shield
And thought of peace.

He unstrapped his sword
And unbuckled his helmet,
And washed off the skin-oil of battle
While his woman watched.

It was as his head
Was bent over the basin
That she thrust the skewer
Through the cartilage of his nose.

He reared up in anger,
And she slipped a brass ring
Through the wound.
She attached a chain.

Each time he moved
Or swung his head,
The pain would floor him.
He became stationary.

His bulk huddled in shame;
He drew his bearskin
So tight around, he was
Unrecognised.

She sang to torment him,
Laughing. Her first notes
Would take hold of his feet
In their bear-paw slippers

And make them prance to her music.
'Come and see!' she sang,
As he was compelled to dance,
'Come and see my husband.'

Sisyphus

Dead, she is piled on his back
For the river crossing.

Before, he rolled his stone
Up the mountain while
His wife watched. And then
They watched it roll down again.
It defied him. Now he is
Carrying his wife's carcass.

He reaches the river bank. Mud
Is thick at his ankles.
Her body stinks from
The buckle of his shoulders

But the gathered crowd
Will not land him. They stand,
Bank-stuck, their words
Sharp like swords, and hold him off.

Slowly, current tugging at his
Bent knees, he turns. Slowly,
He wades back. But they are
Waiting there too, tongues pointed
Like knives. And his wife
Is weighing heavy for her burial.

He turns again.

Houdini

Houdini hangs like a swinging peach,
Ropes twisted and knotting,
Chains padlocked, and limbs caught up
In a foetal crouch.

He is convinced that his sister
Is the mistress of his misfortune
Because his ties were fastened
By his stepmother's fingers,

And he wants to find a goat
He can scape for the fault
He wishes to relieve his stepmother of,
So she won't cast him off like a stitch.

He watched his sister cut free
When she accepted the umbilical scissors
In her stepmother's voice
And thorny embrace,

Not pretending any more
That the blades of severance
Were not hidden in every welcome,
Because she wore her mother's face.

But Houdini, with a look like his father's,
Knew he'd been favoured. So the knots
That grind his flesh, and the padlocks
That staple his chains, madden him now.

He will hang for as long as it takes
To let his stepmother go, and know
She would always have done what she did
And hidden it, just the same.

Malchus

Malchus is hopping mad for his ear.
He has just seen the very man
Who might know the right stitch
To re-fix it, and give it life,
Carried off by soldiers and Pharisees.
The disciple who severed it, follows them,
Dragging his sword.

Malchus collects his flap of curling flesh
And, holding his palm up against
The hole in the side of his head
To stop the air whistling in it,
He hurries off for a place in the crowd
Who wait for Jesus. It is he, who cries out
'Get down, get down, King of the Jews,

If God is your father, how can he
See you dangle like meat, by nails in your palms
And not set you free?
Demand a miracle!' Jesus just smiles.
Malchus, hand in his pocket, begins to pray.
If Jesus is saved, he will
Pull out his ear and be waiting.

Cinderella

Cinderella climbs from the dishwasher.
She has picked the last scrap
Of her stepmother's linguini
From the open pores
Of the metal drum.

With her hands in the ashes
Of the grate in which hope smoulders,
She is doubtful of rescue by her prince
And a golden slipper. She decides
To go it alone and leave home.

It will free her from waiting
At her stepmother's hearth
For a man wielding a shoe and a scrotum,
While her sisters toss her
Fish heads and bones.

She has choices now, and if age
Should outweigh her womanhood
Before she finds a husband,
She'll use a cell donor for the extra
Chromosomes, or be cloned.

Jezebel

She must imprint him,
She is screaming at the door
To be let in.

One time, she must have him.
Maybe twice, to tattoo his elements
To her uneventful skin.

His stain on the folds of her membrane,
Her Turin shroud,
Could lose him his name.

Added to the others,
He will flesh her out. She is nothing
Except through her lovers.

Is he ever going to let her in?

*

Down on her luck,
Jezebel is counting her conquests.
Unknown to them
They have fallen.
She is thinking of selling them off.

She combs her hair and
Applies rouge. Some of them
Are women.

*

Jezebel's head
Has been severed
By a cart wheel. It rolls off,
Followed by dogs and children.

Her body will pack
Into a small bag.
Every broken bone,
Another hinge.

'Am I not beautiful?' she cries,
Her last sentence whispered
From her blunt neck-end
Like the whistle of a hollow reed.

A passing woman bends over the open mouth
And fills it with dirt.
'Quiet, now,' she says,
'Or someone will hear you.'

Malvolio

Malvolio is made mad. Letters
Have undone him before, but now
He sits to write his own.
His yellow-stockinged legs incline
Cross-gartered beneath his desk,
Like sour rain-sticks, pouring,
While his fingers itch.

His sister's honour, he writes,
Is central to her core. He knows
She would never lie or steal, but,
Having appeared to do so,
Only did because her probity
Was somewhat in question.
We must know it is ourselves at fault.

Had we not seen it, his sister
Would have proved us wrong.

He seals his note and smiles,
As letters from the one he loves
Have made him do, in spite
Of spite. He may send
A birthday card with this, to show
Discussion at an end, and truth
Be so deluded.

Hippolytus

Son of an Amazon,
He found himself mothered elsewhere
When his father remarried.
But Phaedra did not have
That blood-lock that must stop
Her wanting him.
She was wanton in her efforts
To bed her new son.
His silence damned him,
As speech would damn his father.
'You must marry!' Theramene cried,
'And your new wife
Will be the flint from which
Your mother's glances fall.' But he was
Not gladdened by this.
'Each female form I think complete,
Each eye, the hair,
The nose, the feet,
Reminds me that I see the witch
In every rising breast, beneath
Each clasp of hands.
The fear that cripples me,
Is how my bride will be
Upon our wedding night;
That I will have chosen
A Phaedra-monster of my own,
Who will betray me
As my father is betrayed.
Better be alone
And take what comes.'

Durga

Durga's four arms embrace
As much as no longer struggles.
Her red palms are pitiless
In their acquisition of anything
Devoid of the breath to protest.

Born as a ball of steel,
She was rolled in her mother's mouth
And spat into a furrow,
Where her father ploughed her in
Expecting her to flower. Now

She prays at her father's rectangle,
To his withered wreaths; she can't love his bones
Because he was ash when she dug him in
And rain has made mud of him.
On the kitchen wall, two foxhounds

Have replaced themselves in photographs
For twenty years since they died.
Home now and hung, she won't
Keep another alive to be tempted
By a neighbour's scraps.

On the stairs, a big-buttocked water buffalo
Displays his meat in a painting.
His life as a pet dogged him until
His legs crumpled at last beneath his beef,
And she buried him, all a ton,

In a hole in the desert.
His horns on a stone mark his bones,
But his flesh has escaped her in pieces,
Eaten up by ants and maggots,
Becoming winged and flying off.

Her husband is boxed in the bedroom.
She thinks he belongs to her now,
But it was nothing to give her
The bag of gravel he became in the furnace,
Devoid of him and empty of argument.

She lays wreaths at his parents' headstone
And sends flowers to his late wife,
Her spite as fresh as her carnations
For those other features; inflection and fingers
Remembered in the woman's daughter. Her petals betray.

The illusion of care with each thoughtful bouquet
Is pointless to a buried husk, but she'll have
The skull for a bead when no one is looking;
A string through the ear holes, its chin
Warmed on the skin of her breastplate.

The bodies pile up to be mourned and pitied,
Some incinerated. She buys another wreath,
She sends another card, she claims ownership
And a pair of earrings after
The sudden stoppage of blood and laughter.

The living go on without her.

Job

When Job was a woman,
God thought she was perfect.

He watched over her when,
As a girl, she took her first
Faltering steps into his church,
Gazed upon the crowd
That worshipped him,
And knew she must belong.

He watched her progress as
She decided to do
Everything that was right.
Her determination was born strong
In her young heart
And he had great hope for her.

Satan begged to differ.
He did not send boils this time,
His tests of endurance
Were more subtle now.
He sent a beggar with blackened fingers
Who reached out and found money.
He sent the maimed and the sick
To have their wounds bound,
Their faces washed
And their faeces wiped away.

He sent a widower to make
The woman his wife,
Whose infants she mothered.
The roses were planted, and,
If she were collecting grievances,
God could not see it in the face
She held up to him on Sunday,
Like a clean plate, for his blessing.

When God took her husband
Satan gave her fair warning,
She got his will in place.
From the look on her face
Even God thought
She was sorry to lose him.
In her grief she was seen
To be akin to God; a heroine.

The father wrote his wishes
As his reason for his will,
He died believing that
His children would receive
Those things of his
He wanted them to have.
Their father's words, Job swore,
Were sacrosanct. For a year
She polished them brightly,
Holding them up to the light
So the children could see
Their birthright shining.

'Never think that I would take
Your share from you for money's sake;
You shall have it now,'
She said at last.
With her promise
Still fresh in her mouth,
Still wet with ink
In the writing,
She kept
Almost everything.

God watched her in church.
He couldn't fathom it;
How could she steal
And pray?
He called to her in dreams,
But she ignored him.
He reasoned with her in
Her waking hours, speaking
Through the mouth of a crow
In her conscience, but she
Sent for a gunman to shoot it
And Satan gave her the bullet.

Now God knew there was
No hope.
Every one of his creatures
Had its price.

Nebuchadnezzar

Nebuchadnezzar has built a temple
Fit for ministers and kings.
He has gathered together the gold
From friends and relatives,
But mostly from his subjects,
For the cost of its assembly. Its dome
Rises from the dirt, as bald
And bleached as an empty cranium.
All they must do is pay to see it, and queue.

Inside, he has erected his idol,
His two-headed behemoth,
For all worship, for all races,
For both sexes, pleasing no one.
Undistinguished, indeterminate,
The figure reclines in obeisance to its maker.
Sexed, but sexless, it is missing fingers and features
With which to identify itself. Around it
Are built vestibules to prayer and science,

To talk, to other idols, to silence
And the inner sanctums of the body.
Recorded, filmed, piped through speakers,
Unreeled on screen, nothing to offend the children
Dragging at the loose ends of the votaries
Who wait in turn to pay homage,
Wanting communion, meant to applaud;
The temple worthless unless
The crowds are fully crowding.

Nebuchadnezzar has made from gold
A thing that once yearly must consume
Its own weight in the same metal.
Unable to satisfy its aimless appetite
The sacrifices and offerings cease.
The dome-idol shrivels from lack of conviction.
The occiput in which it sat, pointlessly,
Flakes in the sun. It would have been better
Left empty until purpose found it.

Its coronet of nails protrude,
That could not pin down
The little thoughts that filled it,
Better off not echoing to the sounds
Of the false prophets that inhabited
Its inner ear. Better off
As its white reaches begin
To scumble and peel, succumbing
To the elements.

The acrobats and musicians
Go home without an audience. Nebuchadnezzar
Holds an auction for the innards.
The success of the sale
Is not reported. The cost
Of the upkeep of the empty skull-top
Is not publicised. Nebuchadnezzar's temple
Has become his tower of Babel
Since accounts of his triumph are now told
In sixteen different languages,
All of them English, none of which includes
The name of his achievement.

Sweeney Todd

All the lies lined up as little pies
And somewhere, a fingernail.

If he makes you pay first
For a shave and a cut of hair,

Have a guess that his slipped razor
Will have severed your jugular

Even as the barber's chair
Tilts you into his meat factory.

You will be reshaped
And pastry baked.

You will feed dozens
From his bakery window,

And one of us is going to find
Your lost fingertip, like a toy in a lucky dip,

Or a pudding sixpence among the raisins
Wanting to break teeth.

Someone will pick out the oddity
And know it for belonging to a body,

A bit of finger-gristle
Clinging to its last message

Like a leftover.

Salome

Salome sways with her drink.
It is many years
Since the movement of her hips
Brought her the head
Of John the Baptist.

She has been a head-hunter
Ever since, but those who knew her
Could not swim in the river of blood
At her ankles,
From another sacrifice.

Such a joke, to have
A head for a dance
As a gift. To know
A life was snatched like a pearl
So she could enjoy

The dead shell in which
The brain sagged. And all
The words the head spoke
Of her pointlessness,
Now silent in its pointless mouth,

Its wind pipe ending
At the tin of the plate
On which it rests.
The head smiles to itself,
Even though its odour precedes it,
It still looks better than she does.

Vlad the Impaler

I love to see the little trees,
Their branches cut, their barbs
Like sharpened spears, be blunted
By adorning heads.
Apple-bobbing fleshy balls,
With eyes a-popping, and ears
To give a starling purchase
Where once were twigs.

And see my arch of bones;
A tangled thing of limbs
As stripped and bare as crows can make,
And leading off, my avenue of stakes
Rise tall above a man,
Each topped off by a face in which
Two puddles for a thirsty beak
Were irises, till thirst was quenched
And holes began.

And here, I roll your children's heads,
Orifices fit for fingers,
Jaws wired for silence,
And play skittles with their arms and legs.

Morgan le Fay

Morgan's magic had already stripped
Fifteen years from the skin of her face
By the time she met Merlin. She was working
On the stasis of flesh
For the foreseeable future,
And had buried her birth certificate.

Merlin, growing backwards,
Thought he'd met his mate
And married her.

Together, they were going to launch themselves,
They would be celebrities.
She would dance and sing
And remain beautiful, invisibly ageing
Beneath the bottled features
She uncorked daily and poured
Into her palms for application.
He would be erudite and write
Music for her, the strings of his guitar
Plucking out the notes, even as they
Hurtled from her throat.

They collected new friends –
Only ones known well enough to perform
As ladder-rungs for Morgan's pretty feet
Would do, her heels like thorns.

But every day they began again, unrecognised,
Having got nowhere, like Sisyphus
Looking up at his mountain. Morgan,

Promising to dance a little faster,
Persuaded Merlin to invest
In stage-time, a backing band,
A photographer and dancemaster.

But the audience still eluded her.
Another little drink and she thought
She'd get them tomorrow. Another little sip
And she could polish the idea
Until it dazzled.

Waking one morning, head
As clogged as a drain, Morgan saw Merlin
Lying like dross in the tangled sheets.
She gazed down at his sleeping buttocks,
His open jaw and unconscious snore,
She examined his impoverished chequebook
And felt cheated. Leaving a love-letter,
She boarded a plane for Morocco
And left him.
Magic, she thought, was all very well
When it got you somewhere.

Scarlet with rage and remonstrating
With the effigy of Morgan
That he kept in his head,
As if she might suddenly come to life
And love him, Merlin festered and boiled.

If only he could spoon her out of his cranium,
Dead, or ended, it didn't matter.
If only he could untie
Her long black hair from the ligature at his neck,
If only he could unpick her fingernails
Buried up to the first knuckle,

From the small of his back,
If only he could unstick her wet tongue
From the end of his penis,
If only he could expel the sound of her last laugh
From the membrane in his ear
Which now so betrayed him,
In time, he would be free.

Merlin is counting down time by its known units,
Devising new ways to mathematically divert himself.
He is sloughing off his wife like scales
To find new skin. He is counting the scales.
He counts the parasites on each of the scales.
He counts the mites on each of the parasites.
He counts the legs on each of the mites on each of the parasites.

Morgan ticks in his head like a clock.

Echidna

I thought I'd buried her.
The malodorous scales
That made up her rotting tail
Had been planted in mud,
As if I expected to grow reptiles.

At least her voice is still.
The primal scream that rent the air
From behind her pointing finger;
The swinging sword of her harangue,
Has died in the pipe that played it.

Do you think that putting
The fleshy pieces back on her bones
You could build her more sweetly?
She is just as deadly, despite
Her uselessly mouldered cadaver.

Now it is her mephitic odour
That seeks places upon me, around me,
In the room, in the house,
To hang its commemoration of her
Like garlands of stinkhorn and iris.

You have up-dug the half-woman
And brought her back in as many pieces
As you found. Are you blind
To the dogs that follow?
It is time to put her back in the ground.

Nemesis

Nemesis is dressing for the party.
She wears her high red heels
And her red silk slacks, she hangs
A weight of gold chain at her belly
As a reminder of purpose.

Nemesis is innocent of the eyes
That follow her around the room,
Waiting to see whose musical chair
She removes,
Leaving them seatless.

Nemesis is introduced to no one
Whose pride belittles their physical body,
Until she meets the man
With his surname detached
As unnecessary.

Nemesis meets this single storey identity
And asks him for identification,
Since his fame has not
Put his photograph
In front of her.

Nemesis sees his black irises
Like two pen-ends, inking him in,
Willing her to know him when
He could be Bloggs, or Smith, or Halibut
But his mouth remains shut.

Nemesis is left standing
As he turns his back, his fingers
Dismissing her, his first words being;
'It doesn't matter,
It doesn't matter.'

Nemesis is asked why. She replies;
'A man of no significance
Would classify himself
In order not to be
Otherwise mistaken.'

'A man of great importance
Would use his name
To point himself out
As having exceeded
His origins.'

'But a man who turns away
Because his epithet was not
Recognised in his features,
And says 'it doesn't matter'
Describes himself.'

Sawney Beane

He likes people.
But it is only after their death
That the relationship really begins.

He carefully chooses
Who to ask home for a meal.
He likes them to live long enough
For six or eight meetings,
He needs a number he can count on
To say they met 'often'. It is the word
He keeps dart-sharp,
Stropped on his hide.

He is still grafted like a stick
To the root of his lost look
At a would-be lover, left alone
To face devils he was too fearful for.
When they had ripped her to pieces
He found her more attractive,
And has been marrying her in his mind
Ever since.

The sharpened quill which he tore
From the head of her dead husband,
Is blunting beneath his balled fist
As it crosses the pages, scratching him in
To that other life as if
He had really lived in it.
Each rewrite makes a longer chapter of him.

Meetings that took minutes, or an hour,
Become days. His imagination, like a blind hand,
Fingers his conscience for boundaries
And finds none.

And this isn't the only body
He's got boiling.

Arachne

Young, she could tell tales in her embroidery
That the neighbours gagged over.
Not a writer by nature
She could still spin a yarn,
Drafted from fiction and picked out
Of the materials to hand
With the needle of her tongue.

Middling, she remained undiscovered,
But the death of a local woman
Made famous by the violence of her departure
Opened up the opportunity of kinship,

Of real friendship, if pressed. Arachne
Took out her silks and began to sew,
Stitching herself in.

Old, shrunken on her bones like an emptied shuttle,
She looked back at her tapestry.
Her thread was running thin,
She could see holes appearing where
Her stories had been fingered by questioning strangers,
And all of her invention; her stolen friend
Now unravelling.

And she, a spider.

Prometheus

Every man depicts himself.
Prometheus, dangling from his chains
Is in performance even as
Prometheus dangles from his chains.

A ball ablaze in oil, swings from a crane
Like a sun, across the face of Xerxes.
Prometheus watches himself, written in
To the play of himself,

In a borrowed tomb,
Having stolen fire,
As prisoner,
Liver eaten daily by

A liver-eater, replenished by gods
For the eagle to come again.
The audience sits out in the desert
On stones, and prays for Heracles

And an arrow to stop
The bloody eagle eating.
There is no one who isn't grateful
When the bird is butchered.

Prometheus watches Prometheus
Drag off a rock from his prison
Attached to a ring on his finger
As a reminder of the marriage.

Tomorrow the play will come again
But he,
He is still shackled to his mountain.

Honos

Honos is having a crisis of conscience.
Her probity, once priceless,
Now has a value;
It has weighed up against her virtue
Since she buried her husband.
A man of letters, his words
Were the clay that made him,
Even as God made man.
He stood,

Sculpted of his sentences.
Honos thought him thoughtless
For writing about anything
That reminded his readers
How she had not been
All there was.
So many of the words he left behind
Once handled in the furnace
Of his fireball,
Were leather-bound and limited
Only for private collectors.
Honos hears them at night
Screaming to be let out and read,
To honour the man that made them,
And remember him
In the minds of others.

Honos has not slept for three years.

But if the weight of her body
Can keep the books shut like mouths,
She will not have to face the sum of herself
Measured up against his feelings
For the people in them.

Lucrezia Borgia

She just can't keep it closed.
Every time her legs part
Her bearded mouth speaks. Its clitoral tongue
Can form words.

It tells of all the things it has seen,
Of all the places it has been,
Of all the phalluses
That have filled it.

Being young, she found no one
Listened to the hole in her head
Half as much as they answered the call
Of the hole between her legs.

Now her labia are releasing their secrets;
Her clitoris has dictated its memoirs
And made itself important.
She has known great men,

But only from the waist down.

Satan

I am the dilemma
In a man's mind. I shift
My body weight along the balance
Of his two thoughts, because man
Has two thoughts about everything,
And with every two thoughts

Come disadvantages. It's me
That weighs up the cost of conscience
Which scurries, furtive,
Around the inside of his cranium
Searching for a room
It can lock itself into.

Some men are born with guilt
Suckling at their breast, in need
Of drawing blood for a feed.
Others, have conscience nailed up tight,
Even before they are severed
From their mother's placenta.

They do what looks right, only
As long as someone's looking.
Their price is as low as a gutter-coin,
And a coin in the gutter will buy me
A whole death in some places,
In others, they do it for free.

I topple presidents. I am the weakness
That makes a man think
The secrets of his penis
Are impenetrable. I am the last drink
That unhooks the tongue
Of the one with the story.

I am the voice in the head
Of the woman who wants,
And wants and wants and feels
Badly done by if she doesn't get,
But hasn't found out
What it is she wants yet.

I am the seed from the soldier,
Worse than a bullet, when he has
Tied down his enemy's wife
And given her life, with his lips
On its little face, and his eyes
Begging for a breast

From the holes in its little head.
Better that it be born dead,
But he keeps her there
Till the brat be born squalling;
Every howl is mine,
The mother's most.

I am the cataract in the eye
Of their source of redemption,
Each man, each woman, blind
To the wailing, open wound of infant
Whose father bred it from the pit
Of all that makes him kill, and woman

Made mother against her will,
To carry, feed and grow the thing
That knows my name. I am
The question that the babes should die,
Because two days on earth and they are
Heading for hell, where I'm waiting.

Don't mistake me for a flood or a landslide,
Nor see me diseased and multiply
What man made. Nor am I fire;
I only felt inside the fingers of the boy
Who picked the matches up
And set alight the trees.

I'd bring him to his knees if he were mine,
Cupboard-shut and wailing for food
Until he's weak enough to listen
Next time. Someone already
Has a bath and a bin bag for the wet ones,
Tied up inside, stinking,

Waiting for morning in fear
At the first noise.
It's not my war when murder takes
God's name in vain. I'm only
Counting weaknesses. He needs to know
The worthlessness of souls;

The hollow rattle of the tin
That each one counts its cost in.
And when I have the sum
Of each of you, and you
Add up to nought,
My job is done.

The First Horseman

> Behold a white horse, and he that sat on him had a bow; and a
> crown was given unto him: and he went forth conquering, and
> to conquer.
>
> REVELATIONS 6

Tented women, denied even faces in daylight,
Or eyeholes lest a muddied iris
Cast a spell to topple a weakened man,
Stumble, legless in traffic,
Blinded by sweat and tears,
Oppressed by man's fear
That his penis be tempted.
And it might as well be a knife
If he not be her husband.

Man is set against woman
And makes her his enemy,
Woman is set against man
And makes him her enemy,
Even as the means of worship
Set God against God.
God against himself.

The disciples do not know
They are followers.
They think they are kings,
Having cut down, imprisoned, tortured
Or suppressed the opposition.
It would not occur to them to step up
On the box of their own great achievement,
And be offered a kingdom.

The first horseman is watching,
As mankind whittles itself down
To the last survivor,
Then he will dismount
And stamp them out like an insect,
Hang his crown
On the branch of a dead tree,
And go home.

The Second Horseman

And there went out another horse that was red: and power was given to him that sat thereon to take peace from the earth, and that they should kill one another: and there was given unto him a great sword.

REVELATIONS 6

The horseman's sword bisects
A father's reason from belief.
Unfettered by thought,
His belief aspires
To become a reason in itself,
And he gives up his boy for it.

The boy bomber is strapped into his kill-suit;
He will go off, spectacularly.
Inside, all his little sons and daughters
Huddle their halves in his scrotum.

They would have opened like flowers
And bloomed, in a woman's womb.
They would have been the best he did,
If he did nothing else.

His father, having seen his son
Used as a weapon, is proud,
Himself now becoming
A dead end.

The Third Horseman

> And lo a black horse; and he that sat on him had a pair of
> balances in his hand [...] A measure of wheat for a penny, and
> three measures of barley for a penny; and see thou hurt not the
> oil and the wine.
>
> REVELATIONS 6

I've measured 'em up. Each one's weight
Against the sum of their intention,
And found their intentions
Leave them lying useless in the bottom
Of the scale's cup.

Their barley and wheat is hybrid for seed
That could not put down a root
To source life and bloom,
Budding its nurselings
For the hungry to eat.

These kernels make bread, but planted,
Their thousands would rot before sprouting.
Voles and mice would carry off
The mildewed nuggets
But the grain be dead.

Man is made indispensable.
There's hardly a woman now,
Who won't be slit from hip to hip
To give her child an opening.
Nor a rose-shoot that will grow
From a fallen rose pip; this
Be no less reprehensible.

If nothing works without
The aid of interference, using tool
Or knife, or pill, to give a thing its life,
Then man be God, but less a God
Since breeding's been bred out.

The Fourth Horseman

> Behold a pale horse: and his name that sat on him was Death,
> and Hell followed with him. And power was given unto them
> over the fourth part of the earth, to kill with sword, and with
> hunger, and with death, and with the beasts of the earth
>
> REVELATIONS 6

The cows are dead,
Bulldozed into pits
With a bullet in the head.

Sooty clod exhales balloons
Of blackened skin and burning hoof,
Nothing left for a handbag
Or a pair of shoes to put feet in.
Their stink beckons, their ghosts
Are windblown like chaff.

All their thousands of legs,
Stuck up from their barrels of bloat
And aiming at God, shout out;
'We're going this way,
We're going this way,
See us pointing pointlessly,
Here for no reason

And shot for blisters,
Not murdered for meat,
Nor poisonous to eat.'

The truck uplifts its trailer,
Hydraulics heaving, and into another burning bed
Tip woolly baubles. They bounce and roll
Until the last one comes to rest,
And from each tightly woollen fist
Falls a sheep's head.

And the farmer faces silence
From the furnace of his fields.
It hangs with the smoke
In the branches of his trees,
It hangs in each room of his house,
It hangs in his barn where the owls
Are speechless with horror, their voices
Gone out like candles.
It hangs from the rafters
Where he hangs.

The fourth horseman watches from
His pale mount. He has no time left
To carry out the offices of Death.
Far quicker then
To set man against the very thing
That feeds him.

Lazarus

Sometimes, God is not enough.
When prayer cannot bring you back
From the pit of your cinders,
From the box at the bedside
In which you are crumbled,
To see what has been done
In your name, and that your children
Are kept from your pieces,
You must beg, dumb in death,
For the power of speech.

It could begin with a word; one of many.
Something written. Maybe that word
Will gather speed and momentum, it may even
Drag its brothers and sisters, its cousins, its aunts
And all their syllables and rise up
Like an echo in the mouth
Of the memory of you.
Maybe this new man,
Made up of your own mind
From the words you left behind,
Will read out your last letter

And make you heard.

The Book of Mirrors

(2009)

The Book of Mirrors

The book of mirrors is waiting for faces to fill it;
Polished chrome or pools of mercury
Are not so demanding. Each page
A flat conduit for whatever images
Are directed into it, sending them back
To the glassy eye of the beholder; a mirror
Communicating objects and people
To another mirror. Stripped of artifice or disguise
It gives us back to ourselves
As we really are; it does not recognise
The means by which we layer ourselves
In all manner of fakery.

The book of mirrors does not hold prisoners,
Although it may expose the cage
Of our own constructions.
If we are ready
It may illuminate the door over our left shoulder
Through which we can escape,
Leaving our old skins behind
For others to trip over.

The book of mirrors is always found by the roadside,
Or on a coffee table in a hospital waiting room,
Or on bookshelves belonging to someone
Who has recently died. It is
Upholstered in brown suede
– As if softened calf skin
Could lessen the possibility
Of being made to bleed by a careless grasp.

The book of mirrors is also a book of memories,
It plays us back to ourselves
So that if we care to look
We can see ourselves as others did,
But it does not make judgements
As others might.

The book of mirrors does not reflect
What is artificial or illusory.
If it shows us no reflection at all
Then our disguise is so complete
That whatever we once were
Is lost, and cannot be brought back.
And the book of mirrors does not care.

Stonepicker and the Book of Mirrors

Stonepicker has been collecting wounds as pebbles,
Stopping often to study a stone in the road
For the slight it might have
Inadvertently subjected her to. Taking
No offence where none is meant
Would devoid her of purpose,
So she must find some insult in it.

And there it is, the book of mirrors,
Lying on the verge and begging,
Just begging to be opened
But only because it is shut.
With enquiring fingers

She lifts the brown suede cover
To discover why it was left behind;
And there she is, naked on all of the pages,
Stripped of her guises, false and otherwise,
As if she were Dorian Gray
Degenerating on glass, not canvas.

If she would only
Lay down her sack of grievances,
And release her stubborn back
From the burden of habit and the dutiful
Gathering of spite and bile as missiles,
The book might redefine her
As someone else entirely.

January

Hades beckons. The River Styx
Has already eaten parts of the road
And whole cars, before receding to digest
Other swept-away organisms that remain
Trapped in the eddies of its belly.
Some of us are left withering at the water's edge
For other reasons, as the bitter cold
Takes a few of the old before spring;
Leaves the rest of us ageing in our greys and blacks
Beneath the skies of grey and black.
Then the gales come. Windy fingers
Working away at window-edges, trees
Giving up their wish to be vertical,

Crashing into hedges that teem
With quivering wildlife.
Snowdrops confound in their masses,
Gathering as if for chapel in their bright whites
With green cuffs. And somewhere at night
A dog barks endlessly, as if
To keep the winter devils away
But unable to guard anything more
Than the one spot he stands on.

Stunckle's Night Out

See him walk.
Hear him talk.
Watch him pour alcohol
Into a man whose woman
He would have. Not laughing,
Just pouring. He would not leave
The poor drunk be.

See him eat, his eyes
Upon the young girl's breasts;
His food escapes his lips
As he stares sideways
At that younger chest.

He feigns an interest in the partnership
Of his unwitting friends;
He'll separate them if he can
With pincers and a tweezer-grip.

The Sign

A man in Japan notices a flax root on a stall
In the shape of a naked man and woman.
He pays a heavy price for his recognition (£40),
And takes the couple home.
Now his home becomes an attraction.
Everyone wants to see what nature threw up
Out of her own belly. They arrive in buses
To witness the marvel – and each other:
People watching people watching a vegetable
In the shape of people.
They think it's a sign, although of what
Remains to be determined.
They believe it to be magic or a miracle;
It gives them hope. Hope hangs
Outside the man's house in the shape of people,
And imbued with credibility by other people.
This engenders jealousy in some quarters,
So, one night, when the crowds have gone home
Or retired to their tents to sleep,
Someone cuts down the misshapen root
And boils it up for herb tea.
The conjoined couple bubble until
They are nothing more than an impotent brew;
Hope as vegetable stew.

Self-examination

I pace the house,
I draw the bath,
I pour the tea, I pretend
A note to myself will become
The poetry of myself;
I prevaricate incessantly.

I follow myself around,
And if I turn, agitated at the sound
Of those other footsteps,
I come right up face to face
With myself, both of us
Astonished to be here.

The Cure

Take these pills, two a day,
And that loose coil
That tangles in your skull
Calling itself a mental process
Or even a brain
Will tighten right up.
You'll not want to stick your fingers
Down your throat again.

I sat, skinny at seventeen but
Feeling the rolls of flesh
Weigh heavily on my bones;

A plate of liver and onions took on a chill
As I negotiated its dietary properties.
Nothing fattening in that
Says the cook, passing over two pills,
Which I pocketed in my cheek
Wedged up against my teeth
And spat down the toilet.
No mood-altering medication
Would ever take me
For ransom or otherwise.
Give me the raw materials; the black holes,
The cold floors and confusion of needles-as-thoughts
That make me feel myself,
Over any stupefying potions
That would turn me into someone else.

Woman Falling

The car has been driven off the cliff.
She sits there, in the driver's seat,
Watching the scenery as the rocks on the left
Give way to trees. The crimson horizon
Turns pink and swings upwards
As the surface of the earth,
Divided by water and carbuncled
By granite outcrops, speeds to meet her.
Over and over again she recalls
The instant that her foot slipped from the brake
To accelerate, in a moment of uncertain conviction
To do, or not to do, something
That might have consequences.

She was egged on, it was true,
'Make your mark!' they cried
From the far side of the ravine,
'Reach for the sky!' But, like Icarus,
When his wax and feathers met the hot sun
Beyond the walls of his prison
And he fell to earth,
Her metal machine cannot fly.
And here she is, falling
And waiting
And falling.

Stunckle Goes to a Party

Stunckle readjusts his balls
Beneath his lightweight trousers;
He is going to a party
Where he expects to see
Many pretty girls.
He tucks his formal red shirt
Into his waistband
And hopes they will know he means business.
Oh, when the music plays
See how he barely smiles,
Oh, when the girl gazes up at him,
Dazed, in some kind of adoration
(Or confusion)
See how he just ducks an eye
In her direction.
He touches her shoulder and something
Beneath her skin flinches. He thinks

It must be the power of his personality
Burning through the tips of his fingers
Like an electrical charge.
The girl shudders a little, her smile falters.
Something is wrong.

Preparing the Ground

Like the portent of doom,
My grandmother flies in from the north.
The magnetic pole of her presence
Appears to repel my father.
He goes away for a couple of days,
And my grandmother splits open
Her face at her smile,
As if taking each side of her mouth
In her two hands
And pulling it apart,
To allow her doppelgänger to scramble
From the lip-noose of opened granny-bag
And step into the hallway.

I watch the flare of her nostrils; the caverns
In which her wind blasts,
As she leads me to the garden
To watch over my six-month-old brother.
Eyeing the boy,
Bottom-anchored by his nappy,
I reckoned it would be two days
Before he crawled as far as the undergrowth
Into which he might disappear.

Convinced of his immobility
I follow my grandmother's scent
Back into the dark burrow
Of the central hallway.
She is raging,
Her storm has been
My mother's marriage long in the brewing.
'You must leave him!' she cries;
This new woman has no warmth
For her son-in-law.
'He'll be seeing *her* you know,
The wastrel, the faithless scoundrel.'

Making a cake, my mother
Scrapes the mixture into a baking tin
But her tears overcome her,
And the kitchen's too small to weep in,
So she sits at the larder table
Unable to contain her wretchedness.

'You must come home with me,'
Says my grandmother, elated,
As if she has won something.
If my father only knew
How she became someone
He'd not met before
When he wasn't looking
He'd never have walked out that door;
He'd carry us away to safety
And not look back at the unloose witch
And her coven of one,
Her spite and her bile
Gut-rotting her into
A stomach-stapling.

My mother holds her face
In the bucket of her hands;
She doesn't notice my grandmother's smile
As she picks up the forgotten sponge
And places it exactly
In the centre of the oven.

Seeing me brotherless
My grandmother brings him in
From the garden.
I have already considered
Placing him near in the hope he can hear,
So that when he speaks at last
He'll bear witness to all that has passed.
But now I see he is dumber than it will take
To ever remember.

My mother beds him down
In the cot in my bedroom corner,
Her own, chipping away at her
As if she were an egg,
To be broken and beaten
And turned into something else.
My grandmother stills her beak
From pitting holes
In the ground of my mother's skull
Into which she pours salt
When she sees me watching,
Not missing a thing; eavesdropping.

She picks me up
And carries me to her bed
In the room my father writes in,
The sheets are as cold as glass
On my bare legs. I'm hugging

My frozen knees in my nightdress,
Wishing, wishing to be saved
From the magic carpet
Of my grandmother's prayer.
'Would you like to come live with me?'
She says, and I ball up all my questions
Into my incapable mouth.
My tongue is helpless, but to ask;
'Can Daddy come?' Meaning everything.
'We'll see,' she replies,
Her face as hard as pyrite.
I know as she leaves the room
That I am losing my father.

I can hear my grandmother's voice
Like a machine
Grinding at my mother some more
As I creep past my bedroom door. Downstairs,
I stand at the black Bakelite telephone.
Someone must tell my father
Before his children are taken.
I gaze at the pages of notebooks
All covered in scrawl, and realise
That I cannot read.

Even if I knew where to find him,
When I place my finger in the dial
And pull, it barely moves,
My finger buckles, useless at the knuckle.
My grandmother's engine
Is the background hum
On the drum of my ear.
My father is too far away to hear
His mother-in-law's tongue
Flaying.

Puberty

There's no disguising them, they're huge,
Buttressed on my ribcage like
Two melon-ends, when all my friends
Are sticks without a shape. They're gorgeous
In bikinis on the beaches,
And gape at me in t-shirts
That stretch across my reaches.
I cannot hide them in a sack
Of shirts that flap like sails,
When the fabric hangs so tent-like
I look as though I house
A pair of nursing whales.
My arms are always folded
As if to hide my front,
But my thighs are beams that hold aloft
The building I've become
And nothing could be large enough
To camouflage my rump.

Stunckle Sings

My life's afloat.
I'm sailing on a gentle breeze, an airborne boat,
My coat is flapping at my knees,
Achilles has nothing on me.

I see compassion, distant once,
A sometimes enemy,
Being kind enough to keep at bay
The barbs and arrows thrown your way.

It's easier to let me speak
To those you wish were gone,
My intellect a sharper spike
Than yours, to hang a head on.

I can rise above the heads
Of those who'd hold me accountable,
When righteousness is by my side
My truth is insurmountable.

God and I are siblings,
Our secrets be the glue,
We know the truth,
We know the truth,
It's not for you.

My Mother

They are killing her again.
She said she did it
One year in every ten,
But they do it annually, or weekly,
Some even do it daily,
Carrying her death around in their heads
And practising it. She saves them
The trouble of their own;

They can die through her
Without ever making
The decision. My buried mother
Is up-dug for repeat performances.

Now they want to make a film
For anyone lacking the ability
To imagine the body, head in oven,
Orphaning children. Then
It can be rewound
So they can watch her die
Right from the beginning again.

The peanut eaters, entertained
At my mother's death, will go home,
Each carrying their memory of her,
Lifeless – a souvenir.
Maybe they'll buy the video.

Watching someone on TV
Means all they have to do
Is press 'pause'
If they want to boil a kettle,
While my mother holds her breath on screen
To finish dying after tea.

The filmmakers have collected
The body parts,
They want me to see.
They require dressings to cover the joins
And disguise the prosthetics
In their remake of my mother;
They want to use her poetry
As stitching and sutures

To give it credibility.
They think I should love it –
Having her back again, they think
I should give them my mother's words
To fill the mouth of their monster,
Their Sylvia Suicide Doll,
Who will walk and talk
And die at will,
And die, and die
And forever be dying.

Harpist
(for David Watkins)

The gilt wing rests upon his shoulder.
The strings that are each feather-shaft,
Stripped down to their core
To reveal the sinew
Of each musical note,
Divide the world of his left
From his right.
And in the silence of that split
He brings his two spiders to meet
At the fingertips.
They glance at one another,
They reach out to touch,
But don't, and flirt.
Coquettish, their knees glitter as they dance,
Each against the other's underside.
Each movement and stride
Strikes a consonant or vowel

In the syllables of their dialogue.
Their dance is mutual persuasion,
The sublimation of their conversation,
And they are so in love.

Message to a Habitual Martyr

You blame me
For all that's wrong with your life
And the ills that beset you,
But you did things too.

I'd no idea that I was an obstacle,
A stone in your ground
That would distract your direction
Or unravel your purpose.

I was ignorant that you credited me
With so much importance
That you couldn't step over
Or walk around.

There are things I could blame you for too;
If I tried, I could hate you,
But what good would it do
To be so tormented?

I know that they were then
And this is now, instead I'll wish
For a small kindness in the future
That would obliterate them anyhow.

I'll step over them, all the steeper
For their accumulated pointlessness,
Because in the face of death
They are meaningless.

There's love here too,
Overcoming who did what to whom,
It's past and gone
And unimportant now, who won,

Since retribution is a tool
Employed by such a fool
As wants to pay back what is done,
Instead of moving on.

And here we walk,
Our shadows long, our years diminishing,
Our chances pass and when they're gone
There's nothing, nothing, nothing.

Stunckle and the Book of Mirrors

Stonepicker's uncle has heard about a magic book
That will give him all the answers,
And show him the door he needs
To move on to the next stage in his life.

He thinks he is ready.
He has polished his cranium until it shines,
Even from the inside so that everything
That passes through its machinery

Is analysed by one of the sharpest brains
In the country. His desire, now,
Is to be applauded in the pages
Of a book that will have recorded
Just for him, his excellence, his achievements,
And the sheer number of his many talents.

He is sitting with a wounded digit
(Having shut it in a car door)
In a doctor's waiting-room, when he notices
A brown suede book resembling
An over-sized bible. The edge, not golden
But glassy, gleams with eager promise
At shiny openings. He lifts the cover
And there is the ceiling of the room,
And there are the walls, there are also versions
Of the other patients, uglied or airbrushed
By the all-seeing honesty
Of the pages. Stunckle tilts the book
Towards his face, braced
For whatever it exposes of him.
He believes that he may see a saint;
That the book will validate him,
And he can hardly wait.

He peers into the glass – but it is empty of his features.
Panic rising, he knows in his stony heart
That there is no way he has ceased to exist –
He has to be in there somewhere.
He tilts the book down at his chair to see
If any part of him is mirrored,
But only a section of rectum is visible
On the spot where he ought to be.

Love Poem to a Down's Syndrome Suicide Bomber

On 1 February 2008 Al-Qaeda blew up two Down's
syndrome women in Baghdad pet markets.

Oh, you are so beautiful. I think I love you.
I see how your skin glows
With the innocence born of your disability,
But that does not trouble me.
You are so fresh and new and pure; I would not sully
Such authenticity as yours.
Please, do not grow cold; wear this padded waistcoat
Beneath your clothes; a gift from me.
In our hours apart it will be
The promise of my embrace. I long
To be with you again. Your radiance,
Your light, and all your separate pieces
Will illuminate my night.

No, I cannot follow you.
My sacrifice is to remain behind,
Have children and another life,
Knowing I have rid our world
Of your affront in being
And others of your kind.

The Problem

Your consideration gives it shape.
Where there was nothing before,
You have reached into the void
And pulled it up, up, out of the black
And into the sunlight
In order to see it more clearly.

Your comparison of it to the other
Thoughts that occupy your head
Gives it size. It is enormous;
A nagging lump that overshadows
All the easier tasks and undertakings
With its huge importance.

Being large gives it weight,
And, because it is yours, expanding
To preoccupy your every deliberation,
You find your shoulders buckling
Beneath the bulk of it, your head
So clogged your neck might snap.

Now your problem has shape, size and weight,
You can properly identify it.
You decide it is a mountain,
Unconquerable by joy, or will, or effort.
You give up and lie down in its shadow
To wait for the carrion eaters to come.

As you lie there, in the same dark
From which the problem first emerged,
It occurs to you that its very nature

174

Defines it as owning a solution.
If there is none, then it is not a problem,
It is an insurmountable obstacle.

The insurmountable obstacle towers over you.
In fact, it appears to have grown.
You beg it to go away, but, being insurmountable
It doesn't move. Instead,
It grows roots and harbours small mammals
Beneath its rocky outcrops.

The insurmountable obstacle has fed
On your veneration of its significance,
And become productive. If ignored,
It will develop a climate.
You ask yourself what to do,
Faced with the permanence of this obstruction.

Uselessly falling down before it
Has left its evolution unaffected.
Better to face it, size it up,
Take its measure and visualise its edges.
Then, imagining yourself at a point beyond it,
Walk around it.

Two Women

Two women sit in different houses
At four o'clock in the morning
In different parts of the country,

Joined by an umbilical rope
That first one tried to cut,
Then the other tried to cut,
But it just kept knitting up
And passing poison between them.
It is a magic umbilical cord,
It is the idea of an umbilical cord,
Really, it is love unrequited, experienced
Always by one at the very moment
The other is driven away
By some means perceived
But not necessarily, honestly, real.
Each woman wants the other
To see her reason, her purpose,
And that she is absolutely
Inarguably right.

One of the women rises from her chair,
Collects the milk from the doorstep,
And ceases to care
About being right.
She turns out the light
And walks upstairs.
The umbilical rope that she shared
Curls and twists uselessly behind her
In the dark of the hallway,
Like a headless snake.
The other woman
Is still tied to its tail,
Being right the way mothers
Are always right.

Stunckle's Cousin

I will not review your conceits.
You are safe enough in your efforts,
Attached as they are to your ego.
I will not even mention your name
Lest your vanity polish and blind us.

You snap the new growth and skin the bark
Of other trees for your bonfire,
But when the ashes cool,
What will you have made?
You break things.
You stand on the fallen trunks
Of those you talk about;
Could you not see over the wall on your own?
Too short, I guess.

You believe you have immunity
In the right to judge others with impunity
As any Caesar would award himself
Before he burn,
Or fall on the knife
Of those closest. Your shadow
Long ago left your side,
Your pride being disproportionate
To your abilities; it could no longer
Justify its attachment.

Breaking down what others construct
Means you inhabit the debris.
When you're buried in rubble

Right up to your stubble
We'll bring on the flesh-eating ants,
Sell tickets and dance.

Gift Horses

Should never be closely examined,
Since a found flaw will impair
The immediate, appropriate, joyful response.
Their teeth are sure to be either absent
Or sharpened and fastened on
To some part of your anatomy,
To be noticed the moment
The giver is gone.
Sometimes we must accept the toothless
Or the sharp-jawed,
Although we instinctively know
That our gift-horse is flawed,
Or comes with conditions
Buried in its hide like blowflies.
Who knows what a ride
The creature will give us
If taken in? Be pleased to keep it,
And should it fall to the floor
Beneath the weight of its responsibility
To be something useful and free,
Recycle and eat it.

Stunckle's Wish for a Family

He cannot wear his sister's dress
Too tight across the chest, he cannot
Marry her history and mother
The orphans he'd smother.
He's a backwards cuckoo,
Not in the nest, but outside,
All around it like Red Indians.

To the Victor, an Empty Chalice

See their gritted teeth and glassy stare
Fixated on whatever it is
They want to get hold of.
Glittering or shining,
Or promising supreme satisfaction,
It is going to cost them more
In time, or effort, or money,
Than they will ever win.
It could be a man or a woman,
Or their own way, or the conclusion
Of a well-thought-out plan.
Their perpetual state is confrontation.
Their lawyer's on speed-dial to secure
The secrecy of their efforts;
The corpse of their smile
Reflects all the little deaths
Behind their ocular pebbles,

That record their success. Whatever it is,
Hand it over. Look,
They want it so badly.
Their whole life is the fight, it defines them,
Without it, they're pointless.
Let them win and fall over
Or continue to suffer their malice.
Let them have it tonight, just give in.
Be free from conflict
And allow them the prize:
To the victor, an empty chalice.

Here We Begin

We are forged
In our mother's womb
Where our voice is given in two parts;
Our means of expression
And making ourselves understood
Is always our parents' echo
In the ears of the intransigent.

Stunckle as Eyeglass

Honour is not satisfied.
Justice is not done.
Promises remain broken.

This man stands before all comers.
He is the cornea through which
He would have you look and see
His probity. His good is magnified;
His less redeeming qualities
Made small as a blisters
In the concave of his glassy arc
Where truth is stupefied.

And from his righteous side
Your ills are magnified,
Your good lost in re-editing
Through the poison window of
His optic skin.

Stunckle's Truth

He'll take your words and make a noose
To hang you from the garden spruce,
He'll change your truth to something else
In order to defend himself.

Black is white and white is black,
He'll beat you with it till you crack,
Lies are truth and truth can lie,
Stones can swim and camels fly.

The Idea of a Dog

The idea of a Rottweiler grew legs
And walked. Its big, square head
Atop the solid, barrelled torso
Looked up, waiting for instruction
Or embrace. The idea was obedient,
Faithful, intimidating to others,
But the idea was lopsided.
So the idea developed a twin brother.
Now, in my head, I'd say 'sit'
And they would, dogs in duplicate,
Each reflecting the other identically.
I could see myself walking the streets
Flanked by muscles moving in tandem
Over the powerful shoulders
Of my synchronised keepers.
Perhaps I'd redden my lips,
Wear sunglasses
And a very short skirt.

Nearly Fifty

Look, I'm escaping!
I'm running out of hours like a clock
On its last circuit; time
Is slipping through the gaps between my fingers
Like beach sand, leaving cockle shells, airline tickets,
Dried curls of seaweed, condoms and old crisp packets
As a reminder that something happened once
In this disappearing life. Even as I stand before you
I'm losing brain cells like marbles. Please do not
Trip over them as you exit.

If I run fast enough I may
Catch up with myself searching
For what happened to myself
When I wasn't looking.
And if I do, what will I say?
Perhaps I'll pull up a chair
And invite myself to sit.
Perhaps I will have accomplished
Those mountains of tasks that drag on strings
Like tin cans tied to a wedding car bumper,
Reminding me of their
Completely unnecessary urgency.
Or perhaps I will simply have cut them free.

Stunckle's Uncle

Onomatopoeia rules the scablands
Where his inner landscape
Is the stuff of sweaty nightmares.
He must walk it daily even as his feet
Trace the earth's crust in actuality.
He is one country inside another,
He is possessed of contrast; when trees
Rise above his filthy head in which
No thoughts (of love or compassion) can breathe,
Internally his desert hisses and spits its envy.
He knows he's somehow failed; his years
Are hanging heavy at his wattle now,
Like necklace parasites. But still he cannot see
That lack of small humanity
Has kept him plastic with intent
To foster ignorance.

Assia Gutmann

I open a book of Jewish poetry
And there's her maiden name,
Translating as she never
Translated me. A child then,
I couldn't understand
The cross-patch plaster stuck
To her concerned forehead,

As she slept in her airline mask
In the afternoons, as if
Youth could be got back again.
I could tell her now,
It's only in dreams
As our skin betrays us.

Her beauty frightened me
Carved as she was of piano keys,
Her hair the black flats,
Her voice on the pedals.

My cloak of invisibility
Was stitched so beautifully,
Even as she made me
The black velvet party dress
I begged her to put a white lace collar on,
So I'd look less funereal
Even if Puritan. I'd no idea
How my mother's face reflected
In the polished coals of her eyes,
So that she saw right through me,
Not to the inner workings of my mind,
But to the wall behind.

Three Views of a Car Crash

1 *Disbelief*

If a tree falls and no one sees it,
Is it really still upright?
If a fish leaps a weir
Is it really still swimming in the river below
Because no one witnessed it?
When a car crashes
And only one of three people remains conscious
To be cut out by two firemen
When the others have already been removed,
Does that mean the firemen were illusions?
Were they born only in the mind of the girl
Who could not, in all logic, be otherwise extracted
Without dismemberment of the metal fist
That pinioned her by the breaks in its knuckles?
When the unconscious awoke,
Went off and had other lives, disbelieving
That such a drama ever took place
Because their eyes were not open
To validate the rescue, does this mean
That the girl remains trapped
In the scrapped and buckled metal,
Not rescued at all?

2 *Red Cortina*

There was an accident when I was
Barely eighteen
And a back-seat passenger in a mini

Hit head-on by a driver, speeding,
His bright red Cortina with sporty spotlights
In chequered covers
Wrong-sided on the road,
Our unbelted bodies hurtling.
He stumbled from his car, dented, lip bleeding,
Leaving the vehicle I was in
Crushed into the hedgerow
Somewhat smaller than it had been.
A bus of lookers came and went
Not even alighting.
At last two firemen hacked off the doors,
For the front passenger whose top half
Rested on the bonnet,
And the woman pinned behind the wheel.
Then they held out their arms for me,
But my legs were trapped beneath
The seat that blocked the door,
Crushed into the concertinaed floor.
They cut away the roof and side
And made a gap just wide enough
To pull me free.

But disbelief in the minds of those
Who had not observed the rescue
Repeats the impact every time I am reminded.
It was as if the accident
Happened yesterday; that other car
Just keeps crashing into me
Because those who still refuse to see
The truth of it, tie me to the memory.

3 *Falling Up*

I fell through the hole cut in the roof
Of a crashed car, into the arms
Of two firemen with a circular saw
Who cradled me to an ambulance
When my legs dragged like logs.

I fell through my father's
Telephone call to hospital
Where I lay unregistered
Eight hours in a hallway,
Unable to put two steps together
And reach a telephone.

I fell through the disbelief of others;
The floor came up
And hit me when someone reached out
But not to embrace me.
I was still falling
Long after they'd left the room.

I fell through six months
And one flight of stairs,
Treading splinters. My own nerve-ended pendulums
Spat and scalded against the pathways.
I bypassed the earth's core
And the crust of Australia;
The sky on the other side
Released me into space
As I continued my trajectory.
Now I was not falling;
I was soaring through clouds
With the kookaburras.

The Reason for Not Being

The six-year-old daughter that I never had
Sits on her bed-edge kicking her heels.
I ask what ails her.
'Children', she said. 'Must we have them?
Look at how many we are already.'
 – I could see she was feeling her numbers
And they were in the millions.
'If we become more, where will we go?'
'They'll build new houses,' I told her.
'But when they run out of space, what then?'
'That's beyond your lifetime' I consoled her.
Although I could see this didn't fix the problem.
'It has to stop,' she said, 'why can't they admit
That we're like an infestation of locusts
That constantly crave to be fed?
Someone must do something, Mummy please,
Do not give birth to me;
Have a litter of puppies instead.'

Poet with Thesaurus

This, said my father, lovingly,
Stroking the beaten-up paperback like a small cat,
Is the book your mother kept beside her
As she wrote those incredible poems.
He held it towards me, a flaming baton
That could illuminate the blank walls

Inside my head. I felt a cheat
To open up the pages and read
New meanings. Shouldn't my mind
Struggle for the words I needed?
Owning each, a solid fruit of labour?
A dictionary will give a word
Its definition and purpose,
So why not use that other book
For the same logical intention?
How limiting such wilful blindness is; what fool
Would damn someone who seeks
To use that source of knowledge as a tool?

Things My Father Taught Me

That I was not less than anyone, or a man.
That I could do anything I put my mind to.
But my mind was a sugar-monkey
That harboured enough self-doubt
To bring me to my knees,
So that the only way left was up
And it was up to me.

Firstborn

On seeing the tiny room that I was born in, in a flat in Chalcot Square

Born new and bloody,
Unpicked from the placenta and placed
In arms that could never
Hold me long enough.

Looked-for like mail,
I was opened, gaping up
And ready for anything. My cry,
So short against the walls,

Was finding boundaries
At the arm's length of an echo
In a room for beginners.
The fates sent gifts

And a white ivory elephant.
Hope brought blindness
To what must come.
Better I didn't know,

Though my eyes must have searched
The faces of my mother and father,
Daily, looking, looking.
I must have watched

Those two big people
Pack themselves into that tiny room
Like two foxes, turning and turning to fit,
And me, in the centre of it.

Letters

There's no justice I can do
To the memory of you.
Your letters read as clearly to me now
As they did when written.
Book-bound they might illuminate
The father that you were, so others see
The loss you are to me.

To the Daughter I Never Had

You have been perfect from birth.
You cried only when I was awake
To feed you. You grew rapidly;
One morning you were a squirming,
Teething thing, the next you were three,
Out of nappies, hand on my knee,
Wanting a story at bedtime.
You were all mine; no one else
Contributed a gene to the colouring
Of your eyes, your hair, your skin:
No man left DNA for you to trace the relationship,
Or for me to regret the association
And his predictable absence.
You have loved me unconditionally,
And without the inevitable battle of wills
When reaching puberty. You fulfil your potential.
Your intellectual promise is realised daily;

You waste nothing of yourself
Even in the little things.
You have identified your special skills,
And the man you will marry,
So I can dress in pink silk
With an obscenely large hat
And drink to your day,
Which is made mine by proxy
As I give you away.

To the Daughter I Could Not Be

You didn't love a mother
Who couldn't feel the same
So you did not experience rejection.
You kept silent those questions
That plagued me about adoption and family.
You were charming to guests
But never inquisitive.
You were seen but not heard,
And formed no opinion.
We were both the dishwasher and dryer
But you did not swear you'd never dry
Another plate as soon as leaving home,
While I have kept my word. You did not aspire
To be more than uncomplaining,
Gracious and subservient,
Whereas my character demanded dialogue
In order to better understand,
And give air to what might fester
In another's mind. If dissent

Undid the soft membrane that presented
A fiction outside the four walls we occupied,
I thought it worth the argument.

Your platitudes would irritate my ear
If we were close enough so I could hear.
Your acceptance of demand without question
Demeans you. You are other than I am.
Your compliance makes you the mirror
On the wall of the empty room in which you stand
Between taking dictation or following directions.
Manifesting no reflection of your own
You are the daughter I could not be;
A captive, while I am free.
My root of sibling rivalry.

Childhood Photograph

My mother is laughing,
Holding me against the bulge
Of my unborn brother, kitten strangling
In my eager palms.
My father photographs us,
All his eggs in one basket,
Bundled in my mother's arms.

Sleepwalking

Unconscious on my feet, was I aware
Of my father's weekly visits
As he came and went?
Did I smile? Did I speak?
Did I feel his arms
Envelop me in greeting,
His breath upon my ear?

Did I watch my mother's face
As she left us bread and milk before
She shut us in and Sellotaped our door?
Did I hear the silence
When she ceased to breathe,
Her head in oven,
Body on the floor?

My grandmother's pickaxe,
Forged in the fire of her wish
To get her daughter back,
Was buried in my father's skull.
I always thought the spike,
In piercing one, found the other
So close, the moment of impalement
Took them both.

My grandmother, not satisfied
To see her prize escape her verbal lasso,
Sent my uncle to fetch us as if
She thought we'd be waiting, as if
She imagined our father
Would release us and lose
Everything.

I let myself slip through
The gap between the floorboards
Of my consciousness,
Until the fighting was over
And the last body fallen.
But the fight just carried on
And my father kept on falling,
My brother and I tied to him
Like flailing arms.

Nesting

If no one breathed
To knock over the house of cards
Of my borrowed home,
I could almost believe
Those aunts and uncles
Were as much mine as the boy
Who was meant to be my brother.

I envied his certainty.
He was planted, complete with memory,
Beneath the bird-infested thatch
With his roots between the cobblestones
Of his birthplace. While I
Floundered in questions
Without any kind of recollection;
Even my name was erased
By some accident of emotional confluence.
I seemed unable to recover
Any part of the child that I had been.

My father, surrogate or not,
Explained the speed of light,
How to tie my shoelaces,
The numbers on a clock.

Our mother died, he said,
Of pneumonia.
Was I hers, or brought in
As an afterthought?
I never asked for fear
Of being borrowed.

I built myself houses,
With books on end across the floor
As walls for rooms
With halls, and gaps for doors,
Or with sheets from chair to table,
While my brother
Puzzled at my need
To make a place my own,
A house inside the building
He called home.

Doll

When I was eight I longed for fur;
Acrylic, wool, fox or rabbit,
Stuffed with kapok, lentils or sawdust,
Or working organs and a blood supply.

Not the plastic bug-faced baby made
For little girls to practise motherhood.
It blinked and cried,
Its wheezing water-belly
Wet its rubber backside.

It was a pretender of flesh –
Even then I couldn't stand a fake.
Its mockery of skin
And painted eyes revolted me;
Its long black lashes flapped
Its lids like shutters as it peed.

One by one I popped its limbs
From the pockets of their sockets;
The fleshy plastic fingers
Helplessly glued at their edges,
The toes, nubs of fakery,
And the peroxide curls like wire
Were dug into dirt with the rest of it.

Years later, an arm was exhumed,
Still waving. The toy corpse was testament
To my rebellion against the imposition
Of motherhood, and if the digger dug deeper
They would have found the bones
Of all the babies I refused to bear,
Buried in the mud at the back of the mind
With clumps of curling yellow nylon hair.

Food Fight

I took control of the parts
That no one else could reach.
I'd found an infallible way to get thinner;
There wasn't a breakfast I'd spend twenty minutes with,
Or a snack, or a lunch, or a dinner.
I really thought I'd be much prettier if skinnier.

There was nothing anyone could do
To persuade me otherwise;
Although my ribs protruded
I still wanted slimmer thighs.
But bone went too, and strength,
And temper; teeth were compromised.
All I'd done was damage
The body of the woman
I was going to become.

Second Thoughts

There was a moment
In a hot bath of teenage umbrage
With a razor blade;
I thought arterial blood
Might attract a stepmother's love.
But the mind's eye
Knew death better
For making nothing but empty spaces.

School Doctor

I shrank from the school doctor,
Balled in slime as he was in asking
How my mother died
While examining my sprained ankle.
He might have known about her suicide,
But pried away my thin veneer
From his vantage point of trusted medic,
His question a crowbar as he
Turned my ankle side to side,
Waiting, as I wept my mother's loss
Brought as fresh into the room as flowers.
I suppressed my fury at his verbal probings
As he attempted entry
Of my inner self. My anger was
A thing he wanted too much
As if it pleasured him, his touch
Sent ants marauding
Beneath my teenage skin.
My instincts clawed me back
From the precipice of him;
His vile dark eyes accompanied his oh,
Too personal breath upon my face
As he studied my reaction to his question,
As if to say 'I'm a man
And I am touching you, I am, I am.'
My momentary sorrow taught me
That in future visits I'd present
A show of mediocrity.
I'd be blank, without a trait,
Devoid of personality
For him to finger and manipulate.

Orphan

'You're an orphan,' she said,
'Now your father is dead.'
Was she just rubbing my father's ashes
Into the open wound his death had left
For me to fall into?
Or was she angling to have me reply:
'But I still have you'?
I would love to have placed those words
Firmly into her ear, like seeding an oyster,
But feared she was removing herself.
Perhaps she was simply pointing out
The severance of death, so obvious,
So irreversible. Perhaps she was making sure
That I had no illusions.

Potato Picking

The old hands are three women.
I step onto the heaving platform
In front of their critical silence,
And know my place; the teenage wife
At the tail end of the conveyor belt.

We rock like skittles
As the tractor drags our lurching cage
Across the endless fields,
Gouging potatoes from the seams

In the topsoil.
Our scarves tie back our hair
Against the dried earth that becomes mud
In the sweat of our own furrows.

Our bare fingers blacken in the mounds
That jiggle and toss and break,
Exposing the pale rounds
For which we are archaeologists.
I am almost unnecessary,
Picking the scraps that escape
The other six hands rummaging.

If one stops to clear her nose
Of the silt that clogs airways
Then I might pick a handful.
I see then, how it works; the chief picker
Gets the biggest and best, filling
The sacks attached to the back of our cage
Like a queen, while we get the rest.
Impassive, she paces herself,
Her languid movements are quick silk
Caked in mittens of dirt.

But one day she doesn't come,
And her empty space remains
As a courtesy.
The next woman down is faced
With mounds of potato
That appear to drown her;
She is fighting back hordes of invaders,
She is flailing against an avalanche
That threatens to topple her.

Her panic magnifies the chaos
Of potato backlog that her friend fumbles.
Suddenly, I am the last fence
Between the potatoes and freedom
As they defeat those who don't wish
To be the first line of defence.
I am nudged into the empty gap at the top of the belt
(This is a compliment), so now they can rest.

At night I go home to sleep,
But in my restless head
I am still on my feet
Picking potatoes so fast
They can roll cigarettes.

Verbal Warning

There are those who believe
(With their heads stuck in a can of gasoline
And inhaling deeply) that several words
My poet-parents chose to use
Cannot be re-used by me
Without accusations of imitation.

So my poems about the bird that is black,
But not a blackbird, should not name him.
All I should tell you is how
His feathers ate light like a collapsing star;
They did not glisten purple or blue
The way that other bird did,
The one I reared from a fledgling

With his black and white patches and thieving
– Yet not a thief, a treasurer,
That wanted to tuck frozen peas
Into the back pocket of my jeans.

And the long-bodied short-legged
Furry creature I wrote about once,
That was possessed of a pungent odour,
Should remain also without identity,
Although twice in my life I kept a pair;
Short-eared humps of sausage spine
With tails like hairy stumps.

Some of those things with feathers and claws
Eat long-eared bouncy bundles
Of downy hair, but not
The balls of spines that clatter
Through the leaves, sometimes
Like something larger.

There are flat-sided fillets with scales
That swim rivers and sea, those too,
Could remain nameless. But words
Are not owned; so here's a stoat, a squirrel,
A ferret, crow, and magpie; a lizard, fox, hedgehog,
Rabbit, hare, pheasant, wolf, salmon, trout, goat,
Lobster, chaffinch, pickled herring and brown bear, all with skin,
Claws, blood, feet, beaks, jaws and perhaps
Preceded by the occasional adjective...

George

He rifles his feathers
As if searching for socks
In the washing basket
Of his breast pocket and wing-pits.
Still sockless
He slides the split blade of his beak
Along each twisted-back tail feather,
Bringing them up almost to his ear
As his nutcracker reaches each tip.
He's as thorough as a man
Who's lost his keys.
He shudders his skin
So his black-and-whites froth
And settle neatly.
An oil-slick glistens from his bum-rudder,
Which flicks up and down like a switch.
He pauses to examine his toothpicks
On the end of which are feet.
Experimentally, he slides one forward
As if pushing a small suitcase.
Step, skip, pivot, stride,
He's gathering speed; he turns again,
High-step, high-step, skip-skip,
And he's dancing a magpie dance
To his head full of magpie music.

George Examines

His quizzical black eye
Polishes its round gaze in its orbit
As it scans everything
To the left and to the front,
While his right echoes the trajectory.
I wonder if his two visions
Are simultaneous, or seen separately,
Each by one half of his magpie brain
Which directs the careful points of his beak
Into the dog meat that I offer him.
He opens it up by piercing and separating
His scissors, and peers
Into the hole he has made
As if he might find something;
His way, his purpose,
A gold-coloured curtain ring.

My Crow

He sits in my kitchen, a dud of a crow
With a creak of a beak
And a sullen eye that disguises
His fear of movement. Tattered by magpies
Smart enough to have two
Stake him to the ground
While three others shredded his balance
And his crow-abilities, he was found

Half-dead and bloodied by some woman
Who kept him in a bath for a week,
Where all he did was fall over
Between walls of slippery pink.
My crow eats and craps like a crow;
He does these small things carefully,
His dignity compromised by tottering
In between his perch and food bowl,
And the palm of my hand, in which he rests.

Slowly Recovering Crow

His heart pounds at sudden sounds
As if about to burst from between my fingers.
His claws tighten on the black leather skin
Of my thin gloves, and I can detect his confusion;
If one foot squeezes, the other slackens;
He is unable to have two thoughts together
And control his toes in unison.
He is constantly startled. The weight
Of his bony crow-body hangs from his grip,
And he settles like a feathered spearhead
In a fistful of umbrage,
His tail straight down
Pointing to the centre of the earth
Where he is heading.

Oscar Flies

He has been unbalanced by other birds
Trying to break into his cranium
As if it were an egg.

He tilts his head forwards
And sharpens the weapon of his face
On the branch that is his perch,
Whittling a waist to it.

His intentions lie in his efforts
As he grips it like a life-belt.

Today he flapped three feet
From the top of his cage to the kitchen table
And back. This was his first adventure
In two months. He measures his progress
In fairy-steps and crow-staggers.

Oscar Sleeps

He clutches his cut branch side-saddle,
His eyes tightly closed against the dull kitchen lights.
Usually at the flick of a switch
He'd be sharpening his beak
For a snip or a bite, watching what approaches
With his critical eye.
But tonight he is not the sleek
Occasionally staggering feathered weapon I recognise.

Tonight he crouches on his perch as if beaten.
His black feathered shawl and chest coat
Rifle their layers so he looks
As if the wind has tossed him.
Occasionally, he sways and must remember his grip.
He snores gently, a little crow-snore.
He swallows and gurgles like a water-pipe crow-child
And something in his dreams disturbs him.
His sleep-talking sounds multiply
Until his own sudden crow-shout wakes him.
Startled, he peers out of the semi-dark
Of his cage as if to remind himself
That nothing can get him;
He is safe from attack from the outside.
But as he dreams
His innards bleed and betray him.
The damage of age chips away at his bones
Beneath his papery crow-hide.

The Trouble with Death...

...is that it's never one death.
The death of my sixty-day crow
Who was already bird-battered and aged
When handed to me in a cardboard box,
Was attached to the happy departure
Of a hand-reared five-months magpie,
Which was still a bereavement of sorts.
That in turn brought home the absence
Of the husband who'd just left for eight weeks in Australia,

Which suggested the idea of his death:
In moments of weakness, a real fear.
The dead crow is also connected
To the death of my father
And the desertion of my mother
Who took her own life.
As I bury my crow in the dirt
Beneath the monkey-puzzle tree
And stroke his glossy corpse
One last time, I am unable to let him go
But unable to bring him back.
I almost have to rip him
Out of my own hands.

Months later, my marriage,
Already rotting on its acrimonious stalk
Follows him into the ground.
And my brother too, who couldn't wait to leave.
Now my internal landscape is little more
Than a bone yard. Sometimes,
In the early morning, I hear the wind
Like the cry of an orphaned animal,
And look inside myself to see my own horizon
Obscured by a confusion of aimless turbinations
Of cremation ash and powdered feathers.
In the swirls and eddies of aborted expectation,
Without direction or purpose,
They perpetually thrash themselves into
One futile circuit of my wilderness after another.

Pheasant Running

Startled, his head rockets
To the end of his neck. His neck,
Since it is attached, stretches
Like a rubber hose. His body,
Since it is attached, drags behind
Like a bag of washing in the arms
Of a short person, gathering momentum,
Bouncing atop two sticks of an afterthought,
To suddenly catch up with the head
And astonish it by swallowing
The intervening length of vertebrae.
Now his head is fixed like a doorknob
To his feathered ball
With an expression of
Nothing wrong at all,
And innocent of the fear
That sent him scrambling.
He flutters and blazes coyly,
A mute flame, his embers
Drop into the grass.
Earnestly, he stoops to collect them.

Pheasant Escaping

It barrels improbably past the window,
Vestigial wings pumping frantically
To propel the ball of copper and green
Up, up, up into the air,
Accompanied by squawks fired from
The fleshy weapon of its panicky neck.
Terror keeps it aloft.
If, for one moment, the bird
Ceases to feel fear, then it would
Plummet to the ground like a falling planet,
Its tail feathers burning up in the atmosphere.

Dead Pheasant

It lies
Bundled like a dropped sweater
Of bronzed threads at the roadside,
As if waiting to be collected.
Only its broken wing
Gives away its identity,
Pointing ten feathered fingers accusingly
At the murderer: That car,
And that car and that car.

How It Began

There was first the small sound
Of a metal wire snapping
Like a violin string inside my head
On a long drive south in Australia,
Me, a passenger.
The sharp, plaintive note
Snagged my attention;
It was followed by a sense of foreboding
That something was wrong.
When we stopped I found
That during our journey my feet
Had become welded to the floor of the car.
I tried to lift my legs at the knees
But the joints where my arms
Were hooked onto my shoulders
Had lost their point. My man
Stared in disbelief at my immobility;
With growing fury, he
Manoeuvred my limbs from the vehicle
And made me stand.
If I had to die in order to lie down
Right there on the pavement
I would have keeled over,
Soulless, immediately.
Weeks later when
This flu refused to cure
The blood tests began,
Followed by a CAT scan
And psychiatric examination
To rule out depression.
They found me sane as anyone could be

Afflicted by M.E.
I could not read or concentrate,
Or walk more than a few
Dead-legged paces, or talk;
I found it hard with wooden tongue
To fix the words in place.
Inertia flooded my veins,
Set like concrete,
And immobilised my working brain;
It would be almost four years
Before I read a book again.
Now, a single question
About sugar, or not, in tea
Could render me senseless,
And sleep was not sleep
Of rest and waking, but a mud
Of the mind's making to wade through,
So that strength and cognitive ability
Were all used up
By the time my eyes opened.
The actions of a day were suspended
For as long as string. Despite my fury,
And all my efforts to resist,
My life as I had known it
Ended.

Letter-bomb

Sometimes it does not take your hand off
As you run your finger
Like a blunt slice down the folded edge
Of the topside,
Leaving the paper bulkily torn
Or wantonly jagged.
Nor does it explode into life
If you neatly excise the flap-fold
With the nearest kitchen knife.
Sometimes it contains an announcement
Of love, or the end of love, or death.
Sometimes it brings sorrow. Or joy.
Sometimes it simply contains hope,
Which might direct your thoughts,
Focus your wishes, and allow
The possibility of a different route
Through the days ahead.
Sometimes the explosion, when it comes,
Is not outside but inside,
Where the real changes are made.

Endgame

I am saying goodbye.
Our war is over. You won.
Or I did. It depends
Which hill-top you stand on.
If you want to keep score why don't you
Count the scars from before,
And the open sores
From our most recent engagement?

I'm walking away. You're clever,
You're smart, you're extravagant
In your employment of others
In our war of attrition.
But I'm not going to play.

We've known one another for years.
We are even alike. But our similarities
Are obliterated by our efforts:
Yours to undo me, or outdo me;
To make me small
So you may claim mastery.
Mine to have you listen, that's all.
You see, for me, the battle was never to win
It was simply to get your attention,
Even if love was out of the question.
I can go now that's done.

For Nick

The sun rises and sets
In spite of your absence,
Oblivious of our separation by death
Or your part in my evolution.
But your shadow remains;
It's mine now.

I would never have given you up
Except you were borrowed;
To be returned to the primal clay.
Had I known that each day
Counted you off like fingers
I might have mourned sooner
The idea of impending loss.
But it would have eroded
The years I thought we'd share;
That necessary ignorance was bliss
Reassuring me that nothing was amiss.

Yet you remain alive for me;
I hear you speak as you commit
The mundane actions of a day; you eat, you sleep,
You exist – an echo from the walls
Of every room I occupy.
The recollection of your voice
Plucks at the sinews of the instrument
I have become for you. That music
Argues with the loss of presence
That your ashes signify;
And our sibling shadows dance.

Eulogy for Nick

If I could have reeled you back in
To the six-month old child
Who was left in my care
For what seemed a lifetime at two-and-a-half,
You would never have lived.

You would never have found fish;
Hanging onto their tails as they led you
Onwards and upwards, your unbound curiosity
Trailing as wake;
Your long-ago axolotls would have gaped
At your trajectory as you ploughed
The world's rivers and streams.

You would never have adopted
A small part of Africa – underwater of course –
In Lake Victoria. You would
Not have been loved and found friends;
The Northern Lights would never have
Illuminated your home in Alaska.

You would not have fished for abundance
And found it;
You would not have formed attachments
With the like-minded in whose lives
You planted yourself as firmly as oak.

If your spirit is wind
You have travelled widely;
If your spirit is water
It has channelled you into us all –

You are still ingrained –
The riverbeds of your life in our lives
Are etched through our layers
From epidermis to marrow;
You are present in each tributary.

If I could have reeled you in
From the ocean of experience that sprang
From the well of our shared origin
And kept you safe from your joy and your demons,
You would not have existed.

.

Notes

STONEPICKER

Dr Shipman: An English doctor who is thought to have killed in excess of 250 people. He was brought to trial in October 1999, began 15 concurrent life sentences in January 2000 and hung himself on 13 January 2004. When people couldn't understand why he wouldn't tell them what motivated him, it seemed most likely that the power of withholding what others wanted was the reason. In this way he retained power right up to and beyond his own death.

Fear: The night before surgery in 1995, I was all alone in a West Australian country hospital feeling scared.

For Ted and Leonard: In 2000, two years after my father died, his good friend and illustrative collaborator, Leonard Baskin, also died. My father's most famous creation was 'Crow', and Leonard was famous for his illustrations of my father's bird poems (among other things), so I think of their friendship in terms of the birds they created.

Myra Painting: This is about a painting of Myra Hindley (who died in November 2002) by Marcus Harvey made out of the coloured hand-prints of small children. When exhibited in public it caused an outcry because Hindley had aided and abetted her lover, Ian Brady, in abusing and murdering several children during the 1960s. Ink was thrown at the paint-ing, which was taken away to be restored. But when I saw the space where it had been at Charles Saatchi's 'Sensation' exhibition at the Royal Academy in London in 1997. It seemed to me that the remaining ink splodges were all part of the artistic process – as much art as Myra's image.

Playground: This actually happened at the school I briefly attended in Yorkshire when I was ten years old.

Stonepicker: A woman who believes she can do no wrong, only that wrong is done to her; she casts blame on others but will not recognise it in herself, and so takes no responsibility for what happens to her.

The Dying Room: Written after watching a documentary on the treatment of unwanted girls in China, and having spoken to childless friends who have since adopted unwanted Chinese girls.

The Last Secret: Written a month before my father's death on 28th October 1998, this poem explains how I felt about having to keep the secret that he was dying of cancer.

The San Francisco Fire: On 20th October 1991 I was at the Candlestick Stadium in San Francisco with friends when the East Bay fires took hold.

The Signature: Shortly before he died in October 1998 my father divided up my mother's books between my brother and me. He opened each book to see if she'd signed it, as she usually did. In one book, he found the cut-out corner of the page where her signature had been. It was an act of betrayal by a friend, because only someone who came to the house, and spent time there as a guest, would have known their way around well enough to find the book and cut my mother's signature out.

WAXWORKS: *About the characters:*

Arachne: In Greek mythology Arachne was a Lydian girl, a weaver and embroiderer of unsurpassed skill, reputed to be a pupil of Athena though she vehemently denied it. The goddess appeared to Arachne in the guise of an old woman to whom Arachne was rude and insulting despite the old woman's advice that she should be more modest. Arachne declared herself better than the goddess, who then revealed herself and a contest between them began. Arachne's work was so perfect that Athena tore it up in fury. Arachne lost heart and hanged herself but Athena wouldn't let her die and turned her into a spider.

Cinderella: A fable from Grimms' fairy tales, the details of this story are often misrepresented (the so-called ugly sisters are beautiful – ugly only by nature, and they get their eyes picked out by birds at their stepsister's wedding to the prince). The basics, however, remain: Cinderella's mother dies and her husband remarries. His new wife has two daughters who dislike their new sister so much she is relegated to the kitchen to sleep in the ashes and work like a slave. When three-day festivities are announced for the purpose of the Prince finding a bride, Cinderella is forbidden to join her stepsisters. She has planted a branch, now a tree, on her mother's grave, and each day of the festivities she asks it for help and is given a dress to wear, each one more beautiful then the last. The prince only has eyes for her, but she escapes him each night to get back to her hearth. The third night he has had pitch pasted across the palace steps and Cinderella's golden shoe gets stuck in it. First one sister, then the other, is persuaded by her mother to cut a bit off her foot in order to fit the shoe and fool the prince. But the blood and telltale songs from the birds betray them. When at last Cinderella tries the shoe and it fits, he marries her and she is free.

Circe: In Greek mythology, the daughter of Helios and Perseis (or Hecate). Circe had the ability to change men into animals by touching them with a wand. She transformed Odysseus's men into animals when they were sent to explore the island of Aeaea where she lived. Odysseus persuaded her to free them by threatening her, having remained untouched by her spell as a result of putting a magic plant called moly in the drink she gave him.

Damocles: A member of the court of the elder Dionysius of Syracuse (405-367 BC). Damocles was covetous of the pleasures his tyrant master enjoyed, since he was a man of such wealth and success. Dionysius invited him to an extravagant banquet where he found himself seated under a naked sword hanging from a single hair symbolising the precariousness of the tyrant's fortune.

Durga: Durga is the name of the wife of Siva. She is generally known as Kali (dark) or Kali Mai (dark mother) in Hindu mythology. She is regarded as a goddess of death and destruction. Usually black, she has four arms. Her eyes and the palms of her hands are red. Her tongue, face and breasts are bloodstained, her hair matted and her teeth like fangs. She wears a necklace of skulls, corpses for earrings and girdle of snakes.

Echidna: In Greek mythology a woman with a serpent's tail instead of legs. She lived in a cave in Sicily (or the Peloponnese) killing and eating passers by until she was killed by Argos.

Hippolytus: In Greek legend Hippolytus was the son of Theseus and Hippolyte. His stepmother Phaedra fell in love with him, but he rejected her. Phaedra accused him of rape and his father called on

Poseidon to kill his son. Hippolytus was dragged to death when Poseidon sent a sea monster to terrify the horses as he drove his chariot by the sea. On hearing of his death Phaedra hanged herself.

Honos: Honos was the Roman personification of morality, truth and virtue.

Houdini: Harry Houdini, real name, Ehrich Weiss (1874-1926). Hungarian-born immigrant who lived his early years is Appleton, Wisconsin, USA. He began performing at thirteen years of age, doing simple card tricks. He graduated to more and more spectacular stunts and became renown for his abilities as an escape artist.

Jezebel: A name usually applied to a wicked, untrustworthy woman. In the Bible Jezebel was daughter of Ethbaal, priest of Astarte (king of the Sidonians). She married Ahab, king of Israel. The prophet Elijah was instructed by God to curse Jezebel and Ahab, saying that she would be eaten by dogs and that Ahab would die, after Jezebel engineered the stoning to death of Naboth, so that her husband could own Naboth's vineyard. (1 Kings 23) Following Ahab's death in battle against the king of Syria, Jezebel attempted to replace the worship of Yahweh by that of the Tyrian Baal, Melkert. Jezebel and many of her Baal worshippers were put to death.

Job: A God-fearing man from the Bible (Book of Job) who was sorely tested by Satan who sought leave from God to do so (Job 1.12). Job lost his animals, servants and children. He suffered such mental and physical pain that he wished for death. At last, having been cruelly tested by Satan in the sight of God without losing his faith or his honour, God restored double what Job had possessed before.

Lazarus: In the Bible (John 11), Lazarus was the brother of Mary (who anointed Jesus's feet with oil and wiped them with her hair) and Martha. Jesus brought Lazarus back from the dead after four days.

Lucrezia Borgia (1480-1519): Born of the Spanish cardinal Rodrigo Borgia (later pope Alexander VI) and his Roman mistress Vannozza dei Catanei. Lucrezia's father and brother Cesare used her, through several arranged marriages, as a political pawn.

Madame Tussaud (1761-1850), *née* Grosholtz. Madame Tussaud's career as a waxwork maker began in the French revolution when she was asked to keep a record of the heads of the beheaded noblemen by constructing their likeness from wax. She later moved to London and continued her work until her last model, which was a life-size model of herself, in 1842 at the age of 81.

Malchus: In the Bible (John 18.10), Malchus is described as servant to the high priest, who accompanied the men and officers sent by the chief priests and Pharisees to arrest Jesus in the garden of Gethsemane, prior to his crucifixion. The disciple Simon Peter cut off Malchus's ear with a sword.

Malvolio: As steward to Olivia in Shakespeare's *Twelfth Night*, Malvolio was duped by a forged letter purporting to be from Olivia, requesting that he wear certain clothing and behave in a particular manner, which in reality Olivia found offensive. It made him appear mad, and this was the sport.

Medea: In Greek legend Medea was the daughter of Aeëtes, king of Colchis, and Idyia. (By some accounts Hecate was her mother.) Aeëtes had imprisoned his daughter because she was opposed to his killing of all foreigners, but the day the Argonauts landed in Colchis she escaped and joined them. Medea gave Jason ointment to protect him from the bulls of Hephaestus, and sent the dragon to sleep in order that Jason might take possession of the Golden Fleece. In return, Jason promised to marry her. She even kidnapped and killed her brother, cutting him into pieces in an attempt to delay her father's pursuit of them.

Jason and Medea had two sons. They lived for a while in Corinth until Creon, king of Corinth, decided Jason should marry his daughter Creusa. He banished Medea but she obtained a day's delay. She took this opportunity to send a poisoned dress and ornaments to Creusa. When Creusa put them on she died from mysterious burns, as did her father who tried to help her. Medea then killed her own children in an effort to cause Jason as much anguish as she could in a form of punishment, before fleeing to Athens.

Medusa: One of three Gorgons. Medusa was mortal but her sisters were immortal. Their heads were massed with snakes and one glance at them would turn a person to stone.

Morgan le Fay: Fairy half-sister to king Arthur, possessed of magical abilities. There are numerous versions of Morgan's part in the Arthurian legends. She was generally considered to have been Merlin's adversary and author of King Arthur's downfall through her son, Mordred. In some versions of the legend Merlin fell in love with and was magically imprisoned by Morgan, in others, it was Vivian, Lady of the Lake, who imprisoned him having learned all she could of his magic.

Nebuchadnezzar: In the Bible (Daniel 3), Nebuchadnezzar was a king who built a colossal golden image which he demanded the many nations and peoples over whom he ruled, should worship. Three men, Shadrach, Meshach and Abednego, refused to worship the effigy and were thrown into a burning furnace. They emerged unscathed, protected by God, and Nebuchadnezzar decreed that no one should in future denounce their god.

Pandora: In Greek mythology, Pandora was created by Hephaestus and Athena at Zeus's request as punishment for the human race to whom Prometheus had just given fire. Once on earth Pandora lifted the lid of a pot (or box) which released all the evils on the world. Hope was the last thing left inside, but Pandora trapped it when she replaced the lid.

Prometheus: In Greek mythology Prometheus was the son of the Titan Iapetus. His mother was Asia, daughter of Oceanus, or the sea nymph Clymene. There are variations in the legends in which Prometheus features. Some describe him as being the creator of the first men, making them from clay, in others he is simply a benefactor to mankind.

He brought down the wrath of Zeus on man by dividing a bull for sacrifice. He wrapped the meat and intestines in the skin, topped off with the stomach, then wrapped the bones in the fat. Zeus was asked to choose his sacrifice and chose the pile of bones and fat. As punishment, Zeus withheld fire from mortals, but Prometheus stole fire in a fennel stalk. (Legends vary.) Zeus had Prometheus chained to a rock in the Caucasus and sent an eagle born of Typhon and Echidna to eat his liver daily, and daily, his liver would regenerate.

Heracles, son of Zeus, shot the eagle, releasing Prometheus. Zeus, though impressed by his son's actions, forced Prometheus to wear a ring made from the chains he had been anchored with, to which was attached a piece of the rock he had been chained to.

Rasputin: Grigori Efimovich Rasputin (1871-1916) was a Russian monk born in the village of Pokrovskoye. He devoted himself to religion, declaring that he was inspired by God. His passionate nature and considerable physical strength added effect to his religious fervour. He adopted the beliefs of a sect known as the Khlysty, a central belief being that salvation could only be achieved through repentance – his interpretation of this was: *'Sin in order that you may obtain forgiveness.'*

He travelled and studied and was eventually introduced to the empress, who believed him to have a beneficial effect on the haemophilia suffered by her son which won him tremendous influence at court, which allowed him to ensure the appointment of the most unlikely people to high offices. His popularity and abuse of power led to his assassination on 16 December 1916 when the Grand Duke Dmitri Pavlovich, Prince Yusupov and Purishkevich invited him to supper at the Yussupov Palace. Potassium cyanide put in his wine first failed to kill him, so they shot him dead.

Rumpelstiltskin: From Grimms' fairy tales: A miller, in an effort to attract the attention of the king, boasted that his daughter could spin gold from straw. The king locked her in a room to prove the claim, on pain of death. Rumpelstiltskin appeared and spun the straw into gold in return for her necklace. The following night, the girl was forced to perform the same task on a bigger room full of straw and Rumpelstiltskin saved her in return for her ring. On the third night the girl was made to perform the same feat with a yet bigger room of straw and in return she would become queen. This time the girl was forced to promise Rumpelstiltskin her first child, as she had nothing left with which to repay him for his help.

She was duly made queen and Rumpelstiltskin came to collect his prize when she gave birth. At her protests, he finally agreed to give her three days to find out his name in which case she could keep the child. He was overheard, dancing around a fire, boasting about his name. When he came to the queen and she could tell him what it was, he was so incensed that he stamped his right foot into the ground, then pulled at his left foot in an effort to free himself, splitting himself in two.

Salome: In the Bible Salome is said to be daughter of the disinherited Herod Philip and Herodias. Her mother Herodias later married Herod Antipas for whom Salome danced so beautifully that he offered her anything she asked for, up to half his kingdom. Salome consulted her mother. Herodias feared John the Baptist who was being held in jail, because he maintained she should not have married her husband's brother, so she instructed her daughter to ask for his head. Having given his word, Herod could not now go back on it. John was beheaded and the head presented to Salome.

Samson: In Hebrew folk legend (and the Bible, Judges 14-16) Samson belonged to the tribe of Dan, and was renowned for his actions against the Philistines. He fell in love with Delilah who was persuaded by the Philistines to discover the root of Samson's strength. Three times he lied to her, but the fourth time he gave in to her pleas and confessed that his strength was in his hair. He fell asleep in her lap and she cut his hair. Weakened, the Philistines were able to capture and blind him. They kept him prisoner until the day they tied him between two pillars of a house to make sport of him. His hair had been growing and his strength had returned enough to pull out the pillars and kill everyone in the building including himself.

Sawney Beane was a cannibalistic Scotsman who lived during the time of the Calvinists (John Calvin, 1509-64). He waylaid travellers to rob and eat them. He was only discovered when one of the victims escaped and led soldiers back to search for his attacker. Sawney Beane and his woman had interbred a family of many. They were discovered amongst piles of body parts which were being cured, and the money, jewellery, weapons and clothes of the victims.

Sibyl, daughter of Zeus and Lamia was a prophetess. Sibyl became the name given to all those gifted with the ability of prophecy. Another Sibyl was Herophile, a native of Marpessus in the Troad.

Sisyphus: In Greek mythology he was the son of Aeolus. He founded Corinth (then called Ephyra) and fathered Odysseus. Eventually he was condemned to the Underworld by Zeus, for exposing Zeus as the kidnapper of Aegina. There his perpetual task was to roll an enormous stone up a hill, only to see it roll down again, forever and ever. Some suppose the task was designed to keep him from finding a way to escape, because he had no time for anything else.

Sweeney Todd: A fictional Victorian barber who recycled his customers by slitting their throats and tipping them into his cellar, where they would become meat pies for his pie shop. He was exposed by the discovery of a fingernail in one of the pies.

The Four Horsemen: In the Bible, Revelations (of St John the Divine), Chapter 6. Upon the opening of the book of seven seals the four horsemen are released to wreak death and vengeance upon the wicked people of the earth, while those marked by seal of God on their foreheads are spared. They are commonly known as The Four Horsemen of the Apocalypse.

The First Horseman: He sits on a white horse; he was given a bow and a crown and sent forth to conquer.

The Second Horseman: He sits on a red horse; he was given a great sword and the power to take peace from the earth so that men would kill one another.

The Third Horseman: He sits on a black horse. He was given a set of scales – for the purpose of weighing the grain, for measuring.

The Fourth Horseman: He sits on a pale horse. He was given the power to kill with the sword, with starvation and with the beasts of the earth.

Theramene (mentioned in 'Hippolytus') was a friend of Hippolytus, stepson of Phaedra.

Thor: Norse god of thunder, son of Odin. Benevolent to humans. Depicted as middle-aged man of incredible strength. God of thunder and fertility, married to Sif. His weapon was a hammer, Mjölnir, made by dwarfs, that made thunder and lightning. He wore iron gloves, and a belt named Megingjard that doubled Thor's strength once buckled on.

Vlad the Impaler (1431–76, assassinated). Vlad III was the ruler of Wallachia which is now part of modern Romania. He was known as Dracula, meaning son of the dragon or devil. Somewhere in the region of between 40,000 and 100,000 men, women and children were killed on his orders. His favoured method was impalement.

THE BOOK OF MIRRORS

If we were sitting in a room together and you were to ask me about the poems in *The Book of Mirrors*, then these notes contain some of the things that I would tell you. They are by no means essential.

Firstborn: In 2000 an English Heritage blue plaque was put up on a house in Chalcot Square in London, to commemorate my mother's time there. My father and mother had lived in a small flat in the building for 21 months; it was where I was born. I agreed to unveil the plaque, which meant visiting my birthplace for the first time since I left it as a baby. I was astonished how tiny the flat was, and the bedroom in particular.

For Nick: On 16th March 2009 my brother, Nicholas, took his own life. Our father's death in October 1998 provoked unexpected family difficulties for both of us, but, for my brother, in the years that immediately followed, those difficulties became a catalyst for depression from which he had never previously suffered or shown signs of, and which subsequently led to his death.

George: In May 2007 three baby magpies were blown out of their nest in a gale. I found two dead and one barely alive. I called the survivor 'George'. He grew up in my kitchen, learned to fly and, when I let him go, came back every night, ate supper with me, played with my three dogs (he had imprinted them as siblings) and put himself to bed either in his cage or on top of the kitchen door. He left me five months to the day that I found him (after two separate nights away as if to accustom me to his impending departure) and I still miss him.

How It Began: In February 1994 I developed M.E. (Myalgic Encephalomyelitis) which initially put me in bed for eight months. It lasted until October 1997, although I have experienced occasional relapses.

My Crow: The manager of a local pet centre took charge of a crow that had been mugged by five magpies because it was an old bird. Crows are seen as vermin and no one was interested in fostering it – except me. I called him Oscar.

My Mother: When the *Sylvia* film was made it was not in the same category as any biographical film that is made of historical figures, or of people who have been written about by members of their own family, or who have written about themselves. Our feelings about our parents represent the most powerful emotional attachment we can have in life; age is immaterial. To have them reinvented by people who didn't know them, to have words put in their mouths that they never spoke, to have strangers imagine how they might have behaved for the sake of entertainment, to have my father's infidelity up on the screen and my mother's suicide as the miserable ending to the story made me wish that the whole film would fall into a hole in the ground and vanish.

Preparing the Ground: This is the memory that caused a loss of memory – I was two-and-a-half – after this day there was a blank of almost two years. When I became conscious of who and where I was at the end of that time, I had no recollection of my name, my family or my home and, as a result, harboured the private conviction that I was adopted. (This did not worry me at the time, it was just the way things were.) This particular memory of my mother and grandmother returned when I was thirty and undertaking a personal journey into my past. I have been able to verify it, but I never retrieved any memory of the following months during which my mother died – nor feel it necessary to do so.

School Doctor: I recently obtained copies of all my medical records; I found in the school doctor's notes from when I was a teenager at boarding school: he wrote that he thought I seemed to be 'an inadequate personality'. I have no idea what his criteria were. But I do know that whenever I had to see him I refrained from saying anything that wasn't absolutely necessary, and made a concerted effort never to give away anything that I thought or felt for fear he would use it to intentionally distress me, because his numerous unnecessary questions about my mother's suicide when I had done no more than twist my ankle, had reduced me to tears.

Sleepwalking: After the time described in the poem 'Preparing the Ground' a few months before my mother's death, I became blank (the only way I can describe it) for almost two years. When I recovered some semblance of awareness around the age of four and a half, my mother was dead and I could not remember my name or where I'd come from. The knowledge that I was my parents' child never returned, although when I found out how my mother really died (ie not from pneumonia as I had been led to believe) when I was fourteen, newspaper articles at the time confirmed for me that I was, indeed, her natural daughter, and my father's also.

Stonepicker and the Book of Mirrors: Stonepicker hasn't seen herself as she really is for years; the pebbles she collects each represent a perceived insult or slight, and she will use them as weapons against the offenders. This poem is about the moment she is offered an opportunity to redeem herself. She has the chance to see that she, who believes she is righteous beyond question, is wronging others in her efforts to cast blame – because to cast blame is to absolve oneself of responsibility. (At one reading of the original poem, 'Stonepicker', a woman from the audience ran up to me afterwards and grabbed my arm. 'I'd no idea that you knew my sister-in-law!' she cried.)

Stunckle is born of the idea of Stonepicker's uncle. If Stonepicker is a female distillation representing women who blame others in an effort to avoid taking responsibility for what happens in their lives, then Stunckle is the male version, also possessed of arrogance. He, like his niece, believes everything is his right and nothing is his fault. He likes to get what he wants.

Stonepicker and the Book of Mirrors: Well, he was bound to find it eventually.

Stunckle as Eyeglass: Stunckle likes to be an authority on everything – you included – and he is always right.

Stunckle's Cousin: Stunckle's relative has aspirations: he is a distillation of jealousies and resentments that manifest in his ruination of others in order to aggrandise himself. He is devoid of empathy, sympathy or the desire to control his impulse to undo what others create in an effort to show that he is better than they are.

Stunckle Goes to a Party: Stunckle's conceit blinds him to the fact that he makes women's flesh crawl.

Stunckle Sings: Well he would, wouldn't he? He loves himself and believes that he is better than we are – so much better, in fact, that only God is equal.

Stunckle's Truth: Pigs might fly too.

Stunckle's Uncle: This is a poem about a man who has managed to get through his life to date without learning anything of love, forgiveness, kindness or compassion. His bitterness exacerbates his failure.

Stunckle's Wish for a Family: He thinks he should have heirs, but as no one will have him he considers usurping some other family – even his sister's – although he doesn't like children anyway.

The Book of Mirrors is based on the idea of examining ourselves without ego. We should have the answers to all our own questions, but if we do not see ourselves clearly, faults and weaknesses included, our answers will be distorted by our vanities and will fail to resolve those questions.

The Cure: It has always been vital to me to know that whatever I am feeling is real, so that I can deal with it. Although mood-altering drugs may be necessary for some (on medical grounds), they don't feature in my life. When I was anorexic and bulimic as a teenager I was prescribed anti-depressants – although I wasn't depressed. I feared they would alter who I was and I was fighting to be in control of that (which is why I was bulimic, not depressed). At the time I didn't know that my mother's suicide was contributed to by the fact she was prescribed anti-depressants which exacerbated her symptoms (she was allergic to them and because they went by another name in the UK, this wasn't picked up on). Spitting out those pills (and flushing the rest) was, in my case, probably the best thing I could have done, since I may have a genetic predisposition to some medication – as my mother did.

The Idea of a Dog: When *Tatler* (UK) published this in their February 2005 issue they put me in a minute skirt flanked by two Rottweilers for a double page spread.